Dear Consul Lauture Jacques,

Thank you for your service
and devotion to a better Haiti. Let these
pages refuel our collective obligation
toward a prosperous homeland.

— Ralf

THE WEIGHT
OF MY
DREAM

THOUGHTS ON REBUILDING A PROSPEROUS HAITI

RALF S. RHO

**TWOMD
PUBLISHING**

*"For I know the plans I have for you," declares the Lord,
"plans to prosper you and not to harm you,
plans to give you hope and a future."*

—Jeremiah 29:11 NIV

To all the people who are helping me carry the weight of my dream: Luc, Jeanne, Dapheline, Rolf, Nora, my long list of ancestors and extended family.

✦ ✦ ✦

To my heartbeats:
Tyrese, Amy and Ralf, Jr.

✦ ✦ ✦

And, finally, to Haiti.

CONTENTS

✦

✦

PREFACE

A STRETCH OF blue ocean lays a short distance between Haiti and the United States. A contrast of two extremes, a perfect illustration of the idea of the tale of two cities—two countries that are politically and economically entwined, the audacity of one's progressive founding fathers indirectly expanding the other's size through the Louisiana Purchase. I knew that one day I would be reunited with my dad, who thought our family could best work our destiny by being in Boston. I had played that day in my head several times before it arrived. As our flight continued north, the landscape of America unfurled below me like nothing I expected. I still have vivid memories of the snowy November day in 1998 when I migrated to the United States, an adolescent entering a culture shock that, for the longest while, would continue to nurture an insatiable nostalgia for my days as a child running barefoot and carefree in Haiti.

Moving to Boston was not my choice. Years of political instability and recurring economic depressions, two common dilemmas, more like curses that continue to chase generations of great brains away from the motherland, led my parents to make the decision. Like many other Haitians scattered across the diaspora, I could never let go of those feelings of nostalgia. I always nurtured the hope of returning to Haiti. During those first years in the United States, emotions would run high, those feelings of having been abducted from my youthful happiness, or perhaps from unforeseen calamities and pains. I struggled, though I made the most of the opportunities offered to me. Yet my accomplishments somehow made winter days harder, the cold made more biting by a deep longing and feeling of absence from my homeland, a country still emerging from the economic and social devastation of the massive 2010 earthquake.

Growing up in Valère were the good old days. Children would sit under the light of the streetlamp to study for tests. Hibiscus bordered the sidewalks to launch their light and burning perfume under the anxious sun of every day. One could not resist the charm, the natural landscape's rare beauty that could have added value to our tourism industry. In the summer, my neighborhood friends and I would meet on the field behind the open-air market to play soccer until our hair was scorched by the sun, cutting out the features of our faces, filtering channels of sweat until our charms were no more. In the silence of the night, the trees danced quietly; waves of heat rose from the grass in my backyard, narrating their complaints and pains. This scenery was the tepidness of July.

Vacationing in Trouillard, a province town in Camp-Perrin, I played marbles in the dirt, dominoes under the orange tree, ate mangoes for breakfast and grilled corn on the cob for dinner, bathed in irrigation ditches to shorten the long, dry days of August. With no electricity to provide entertainment, we played catch, hide-and-seek, and tug-of-war before going to bed. In the perfect nocturnal tranquility, the stars in the sky would swell and brighten, the flowers fold and shrink. The wind would snore madly along with the sweet songs of the locusts. But my favorite vacation days were always spent in Port-Salut, where Dad and I were born and he and Mom married. I always loved the flame of the sun on the blue water, undulating and warm, hitting the sandy beach at the perfect angle.

With those memories intact, I returned to Haiti five years ago full of bright optimism, launching myself into the fight for a more prosperous country.

I accepted an advisory role on the presidential campaign to elect Jovenel Moïse. My experience in local government in Fall River, Massachusetts, and politics in general, would prove serendipitous. Before my return, I would visit Haiti every year, sometimes twice a year, sunbathing in ninety-five degrees daily, swimming under each string of sunlight and drinking sweet coconut water on many of our fine beaches. Yet this time it was different; I realized that if leaving the Haiti of my childhood behind was to have been *for* anything, *meant* anything, I would have to live for the future of Haiti, steering every moment toward a dream bigger than myself. Inspired by my parents' examples of community building, I embarked on a new journey: finding my purpose in the service of the motherland.

During my time on the campaign trail, I rediscovered a Haiti of endless possibilities and opportunities. I saw such raw beauty traveling through many parts of the country. I also learned that the poverty of our people is real. I listened attentively to many stories of destitution and misfortune. Even in the diaspora, our compatriots' stories reminded us of the constant suffering our brothers and sisters endured in search of a better life on distant shores. Nonetheless, I have seen countless examples of our solidarity and community, our hunger for growth.

Shortly before the election, Haiti suffered another catastrophe. After snaking its way through the Atlantic and the Caribbean, Hurricane Matthew landed with full force on our southern shores. It was the strongest to hit Haiti in more than fifty years. The nation's south coasts almost collapsed under the wrath of the storm. The country was utterly unprepared, allowing evil to go unchecked and desperation to propagate. We lost nearly all the progress that had been made in the recovery from the deadly earthquake six years before. On the third day, the government announced the postponement of elections—the second time in 2016. First had come a political emergency, then another natural disaster. It felt like the things that needed to happen to further Haiti were always being delayed. Our best plans keep getting sidelined by one rare but ultimately foreseeable event after another.

After the election, I became an adviser to the president, a unique position that armed me with invaluable experience in which I learned that our government continually imposes prescriptions that treat symptoms without addressing the root causes. I took a cabinet position with the hope of contributing to Haiti's brighter future only to discover our government was not focusing energy on solving problems but instead creating new ones. Our elected officials seemed to forget that other countries functioned well on reason, science and justice. Too many of our elected officials were willingly dishonest at all levels. Even when their deceits would recede from the entire nation for thirty years, their political delinquency would keep the Haitian people in extreme poverty, and their corruption would continue to steal from and ruin every generation's dreams and aspirations.

I have found the following to be true in politics: Politicians all too easily will climb their way up the ladder by bribing, stealing, lying, cheating and manipulating the trust that others grant them in the name of getting ahead for its own sake. They will promise prosperity with an open and outstretched hand while gripping personal gains from the public coffers in a closed fist behind their backs.

But the emerging era of science and technology has increased the hunger for change in Haiti. As Moïse came to the presidency, the strength of the Haitian national consciousness was beginning to be felt across continents, defying the odds and breaking barriers to engage the diaspora's greater influence.

A collective movement took shape; a wind of change blew, allowing the youth to connect the dots using social media. They assembled into groups to advocate for a new Constitution and a democracy in which everyone played by the same common-sense rules. They pressured for the modernizing of government technology infrastructure. They asked for new leadership, a more robust government that could solidify systems to change the course of a nation vulnerable to wannabe leaders who promised quick fixes and a people who resisted illogical controls and pushed for innovations. They demanded accountability and more sensible state regulations that secured a better society based on human welfare. A state focused on tolerance without neglecting the pressing need for strong justice. A country that rid impunity for elected officials and the wealthy, a community of peace, security and prosperity, a state where everyone could live well, work properly and raise a family in dignity.

During that time, a ray of hope gleamed in all corners of the country, proclaiming that a new Haiti was on its way, one that no one could thwart. It announced a country where all forces harmonize toward one objective. In turn, this harmony would allow us to overcome all the challenges that have plagued us for decades. It was clear that whatever we want as Haitians, we always achieve when we put politics aside and rally our strengths. Soon, my voice joined with the whispers of the silent majority, a chorus of uprisings catching wind of the government's many broken promises.

On July 6, 2018, the announcement of the ending of fuel subsidies forced hundreds of protesters to set up roadblocks throughout the country and endorse widespread looting of private businesses and properties. Immense columns of smoke towered up as tires burned on the streets, the smell choking and fetid. People died during the chaos. I took a public stance against the administration, which placed me at the intersection of power, purpose and politics.

My short and sharp statement echoed a loud tune of dissent across the entire nation, marking the beginning of my political activism. It was true then, even more accurate today. It is sound advice to all aspiring leaders. However, my position ignited much resentment from other cabinet members at the time. The most significant barrier to our political evolution

"When you are not creating jobs for the people, you cannot upsurge the cost of living against them."

is our intolerance of dissension, whether or not it is valid. Our leaders do not listen to sound advice except when it erupts from the echo chamber. They recast criticism as espionage and dissent as treason. The leadership refused to accept the dire impacts of increased fuel costs on the population at large, as I pointed out in my tweet. It dawned on me that the sincerity in one's position, the courage found in one's voice, can influence, inspire and incite change.

The events of that day in July placed our country yet again at the center of political turmoil. International news organizations tend to tell Haiti's same old story, a description of a country with great promise where fate always seems to misdirect elected officials. To say that Haitian history can be looked at as a cycle of hope and cynicism, to see the status quo as permanent failures to see the larger picture of our collective resolve. Haiti has of late been consistently pushing back against the dual darkness brought on by political misdeeds, foreign entanglements and natural disasters.

By the beginning of 2020, I had grown more frustrated and impatient with the current administration, a disappointment that had been rising steadily. The administration was ruling by decree while lacking the legitimacy to lead; it frequently published regulations that would spark outrage only to recant them later, misbehaving like children who take pleasure in upsetting their parents. The testimonials of public officials alleging the institutionalization of gangs in the country, state-sponsored brutality and systemic repression of the youth protesting against insecurity aggravated me to the core. Each of my tweets and public statements became sharper than the last. I was desperate for better leadership. I awaited a break from the habitual political rhetoric and miscalculated promises to restore the state's integrity and honesty. But the president's words would provide no relief. Every speech was a compilation of the former, uninspiring and insensitive to current events. If these were, by design or tragic default, the president's idea of what we deserved as a nation, we—my generation—would rather take it upon ourselves to rebuild a better Haiti.

No one can dissuade me from the belief that Haiti will change soon. My experience, torment, suffering, and all my inspirations continue to strengthen my hopefulness that the country will change course toward the road to prosperity, just as our ancestors dreamed. Serving my country is no longer an option. It is a moral obligation, as it rests on my generation to create this new Haiti we all desire. It should not be dependent on any president's power or personality, but on the very authority we assign to people who make our institutions work for us.

A world-class education, a twenty-first-century and competitive economy, sustainable infrastructure and energy, an affordable health-care system and more are waiting for us to embrace as our own. Several other countries in the most impoverished conditions and with the worst political records have managed to alter their course. I believe Haiti's chances of success are far greater because the development models have already been tested and improved upon in other places and are there for us to adapt and adopt. We want to live well, work freely and raise the next generation in a reality where their futures are obtainable, not on continued promises that fall to nothing after each election. Of that, we have all had enough.

The past mistakes, natural disasters, political violence, foreign oppression and corruption that have become the drivers of our history do not have to remain impediments to our growth. The old rules, which we are breaking faster than new ones can be written, only afford us the opportunities to narrate a better destiny. In *The Weight of My Dream*, I propose a five-part blueprint to rebuilding the Haiti of our dreams through leadership, empowerment, accountability, transparency and justice, the fundamental tenets for any working democracy. This book encapsulates my unwavering optimism as cultivated by my personal experience, culminating in a vision too critical to contain. I hope it serves as a source of inspiration for my generation to rebuild a better country.

LEADERSHIP

An experiment that will lead generations of Haitians to a dream of boundless realities—a country dedicated to the mighty proposition that united, we are stronger.

HAITI NEEDS A new form of leadership: an experiment that will lead generations of Haitians to a dream of boundless realities, a country dedicated to the mighty proposition that united, we are stronger. Our founding fathers personified this exemplary leadership, impelling France, with one of the greatest armies in the world, to surrender to them in November 1803. Their vision and ideals of liberty positioned Haiti as the first Black republic in the new world, a leadership that allowed us to carry the torch of freedom to our neighbors and many other oppressed nations.

It is not mere gratitude that led many neighboring countries to continue to revere our founding fathers' accomplishments. Haiti has always bred leaders to carry their visions beyond their age and frontier. Leaders such as Toussaint Louverture, a prudent strategist born with a dream, planted the tree of our freedom so that its roots would continuously grow more profound and more robust. His extraordinary efforts at reaching across racial lines and social class set him apart from his contemporaries. His vision of an independent country of equals was ahead of his time.

Then, Jean-Jacques Dessalines blew a ferocious and contagious wind of liberty through the entire island and successfully led an army against subjugation. Catherine Flon sewed together two pieces of sacred cloth to symbolize a republic above all oppression. Henri Christophe, a sophisticated, intelligent leader, established our first political system, moral codes and good governance. He went so far as to leave the Citadelle Laferrière and the Sans-Souci Palace as examples of the extraordinary things we can achieve.

Alexandre Pétion, a champion of democracy, emphasized the importance of intellectual development as a birthright. He knew that education was indispensable for the creation of a rational populace and a Haitian culture. Then his successor, Jean-Pierre Boyer, reunited the country, after more than a decade of separation as North and South, notwithstanding all foes, and reminded us that our strength lies in our union as a people, in learning to live with one another despite our differences.

Our founding fathers stood up for what was right, waged wars and fought for moral reasons; they aspired to equality and lured followers through righteousness.

Their bloodlines and leadership continue to surpass national ties to help other countries rise to their moments, to reach a higher dimension in securing their own paths toward the greater good. There have been many world leaders of Haitian ancestry who have affected change in their immediate environment. Leaders like José Francisco Peña Gómez, who surpassed the limitations created by an oppressive state to reshape the course of democracy in our neighboring Dominican Republic, and others like Jean-Baptiste-Point du Sable, who is recognized as the founder of the great city of Chicago, and William Edward Burghardt (W.E.B.) Du Bois, a civil rights activist who addressed the wounds of racial sins fighting for social justice for Blacks in the United States.

When we Haitians threw off the chains of slavery, it was an active mass participation, all-hands-on-deck, guided by outstanding leadership to chart the ship into the future, defeating British, Spanish and French troops to reform our political and social structure. We must always draw wisdom from our founding fathers' examples of leadership. They must be the hallmarks of all the hopes we cultivate for a better Haiti, a country to drive future generations to a dream of boundless realities.

❖ ❖ ❖

And yet it has been over two hundred years of relentless struggle, and we have still to realize our ancestors' dreams because Haiti's destiny has been in the hands of unscrupulous leaders, those who continuously turn a blind eye to the country's condition. Over time, our suffering, exploitation and poverty have devoured our reasoning, our humanity, our compassion as people. We have lost faith in the ways of government.

We did not get here by accident, however. Our social problems, underdevelopment and political instability are a collection of the great sins of corruption and mismanagement the leaders before us have left behind. Their heritage has oppressed our hope, forced us to live in poverty, driven our young people to leave the country. Still, our greatest agony is in the story that those leaders tell to convince themselves that they love Haiti.

I have seen how they play their game. For those in elected office, debates seem to take on a hypothetical quality: cost versus effectiveness. They too often become removed from their actual human impact. This reality is the root of corruption and bad governance all over the world. Like many governments worldwide, Haiti has isolated and disconnected itself from its people; political expediency aside, the people become irrelevant except for the few months before an election.

I dream of a country with a brand-new form of political leadership, a generation of men and women armed with not only the intelligence but the courage to do what is right in the face of adversity. Leaders who will nurture a moral, spiritual and legal authority to challenge and reform the status quo, promote change and action against inertia, call the nation back to the ideals of democracy and forward to a collaborative vision. Men and women who will not be afraid to tell the truth, even when it threatens their own interests. Leaders who will not apply bandages on the symptoms but attack the country's diseases to the bone. Leaders who will not protect personal, narrow, petty interests, but force the government to make significant decisions, even those that are unpleasant, when they are in the people's best interest. I dream of men and women who will accept when they err and have the will to correct their wrongdoings, leaders full of the awareness and wisdom to cooperate with others, even those who do not always agree with them. Leaders who will avoid the excesses of idealism and the conveniences of opportunism to redirect the nation toward prosperity in moderation.

We renew our hope for this dream after each election in Haiti. A fountain of fresh ideas springs forth as if a tidal wave of good fortune is on the way. The sun seems to shine a bit brighter when we welcome each new president. At least, that is the way I remember feeling at a young age, when our first democratically elected president, Jean-Bertrand Aristide, was elected. The majority of us, then, saw his ascension as an opportunity to bury the demons of our past. We thought he would be the savior who would restore our human decency and elevate us to newer heights in acquiring judicial and economic standards. Decades and many elections later, we were still looking for that leader.

The results of the 2016 presidential elections confirmed the same reverberations: a swift, exhilarating sweep of victory that carried us over. No other candidate was as articulate in proposing a coherent vision. We navigated through troubled waters campaigning for almost two years, the most extended in our history. The traditional politicians seemingly were locked in a death spiral to outdo the others in every outrageous behavior to gain or retain power, as though their ostentatious political assaults would obscure their lack of a plan to lead the nation. We bore the kind of adversity that no man aspiring to Haiti's presidency had ever had to endure.

I can still recall my first moments with Jovenel Moïse in his office in May 2015. At first glance he was a skinny man, far from a commanding presence. Yet he embodied a wit that could move mountains, coupled with a persuasive tenor and a touching life story. From the day I met him, his humility and dedication to Haiti had inspired me; never had I imagined such a stark contrast could exist between the man *seeking* power and the man *in* power. At the height of the excitement that came after the election's official results, President Moïse lost sight of what truly mattered: implementing a national plan for his first hundred days in office. Instead, he enjoyed the celebratory moments, which clouded his judgment, rendering him unable to establish distinctions between genuine compliments and deceitful ploys made by his opponents.

To me, his election afforded us an opportunity to set the tone for significant reforms, a welcome break from politics as usual and dishonest and craven calculations to restore integrity and honesty to the public sphere.

February 7, 2017, inauguration day, was long overdue. It marked a historical date highlighting a long trail of political moments in Haiti. I had expected a well-organized exhibition that exceeded human perfection, an invisible, working intelligence to orchestrate the parade processions to administer the solemn oath of office, those democratic traditions that should inspire confidence in our government. Instead, I was frustrated by the gulf between what was and what could have been. The progression was total disorder, the delay and the misinterpretation of our program for the day leading to a disrespectful admission of the new president into the higher halls of power. Stories of prior administrations' inauguration days are recounted as commemorations of victory, those beginnings of new presidential terms. Through this experience, I quickly discerned that the events were never triumphs for anyone, even less so for the people.

By the time I entered the overcrowded chamber of Parliament, where the president-elect would be sworn in, the level of ineptitude got under my skin, creating an unbearable discomfort. It was nearly as if we were at war with excellence. I understood that it made sense for a president-elect to take the oath of office in a structure representative of one of the three branches of government. Other democratic nations do the same. But I failed to grasp why the Senate president was the one to administer the executive branch's oath. The speaking of that oath of office is a sacred and solemn experience, the acceptance of a constitutional mandate for the new president, who pledges to uphold the Constitution and affirm his promise to abide by the laws that govern our country. In that respect, only the judicial branch has the legal authority to administer such an oath. Having the legislative branch recognize the executive branch's authority is to indirectly suppose that Parliament is more in command than the latter. This oversight has probably been the basis for the long, contemptuous struggle, the never-ending friction between the two branches.

The inauguration ceremonials led us to the National Palace—the landmark that has housed the office of the president since the 2010 earthquake—that same day. It would be the third time I would enter the place meant to serve as the seat of government and a presidential family residence. My first time was as a teenager, contemplating the white edifice and wishing to live there one day. This probably is the dream of many children, in many countries, who start their lives, as I did, with huge aspirations and a strong optimism that ensuring a bright future for their nation was far more possible than we imagined. I could still picture the huge columns that once rose to the ceiling and the double staircase that led to the second floor. Now, standing across from the empty lot where once stood Georges Baussan's classical design as a symbol of our freedom, the strength of our presidency, the collective pride of many generations, my heart wept.

I reported for my first day of work following the inauguration hoping I would rekindle my childhood dream. We had much work to do to foster, promote and develop the welfare of the nation. However, being a member of a new presidential administration comes with both advantages and shortcomings. One suddenly has more friends and relatives than one could ever imagine. Everyone makes recommendations and calls in favors. Even when both are advanced with the best intentions, the process of filling top positions often devolves into a mess of infighting, with many going to individuals because of political favors rather than merit. The executive branch of the government has almost no institutional capacity to recruit worthy appointees. Political appointment-making was influenced heavily by patronage demands originating in the Parliament and the political parties.

When the president chose former Minister of Finance Wilson Laleau as his chief of staff, the infighting for the position grew worse, just like a tale of various disagreements, setting an upsetting tone that would affect the administration's direction for years to come. We inherited a government of complexity that, to be effective, would require discipline and coordination, which could only be achieved by the presence of a central harmonizing point, someone who could unite the administration, command its respect: a strong chief of staff to oversee the synchronization. With all due respect to Mr. Laleau's academic achievements and regard to his remarkable service to the country, he belonged to another time. From day one, he epitomized a controversial figure who could not get the job done. Not only could he not provide the executive office of the president with insulation from quick, uninformed resolutions, but from the way he patronized the president to his uninspired recommendations, he failed to create an efficient structure of reporting and decision-making.

I lived through much suspense while navigating the Palace's complex environment of political intrigue weaved from dozens of characters in shades of altruism and opportunism. Each day brought something new, intensifying a dark saga of a quest for power without the wisdom of experience from those who had borne the responsibilities of being a presidential adviser. By the time the Moïse-Lafontant government was formed, I had already made many foes because I refused to participate in the culture of nepotism and cronyism that promoted corruption and fueled a patent lack of fairness to our public service, undermining our institutions' quality.

Public service is a privilege. It should not serve selfish interests. Considering the failures of the past, selecting the right members to form a cabinet is essential in setting new leadership apart from its predecessors. The right cabinet lays the foundation for a successful term, and there is only a short window of time to get it right. It is the mark of any administration in answering *whom* they serve, *how* they serve, and *why* they serve. Haiti has millions of brilliant minds. Therefore, we should base our choices on the total person, not their academic achievements or political connections alone. The scope of government expanded and the technical complexity of its functions increased; therefore, the qualifications for appointees must change to include technical and policy expertise as well as political loyalty to the president. We must always vet cabinet members thoroughly for a provable track record of expertise, a solid moral reputation and unshakable trustworthiness. Those criteria are particularly important; some of those in line for important positions had, in the past, been agents of destruction, had collaborated and conspired to nurture political instabilities and stolen countless opportunities from past and future generations. Haiti's government needed a cabinet made up of individuals with integrity, competence and passion—a team of public servants recruited and promoted based on ability and merit to manage a rather large and complex public sector. President Moïse's experience was no different from that of his predecessors. Now his cabinet embodied traits of the very corruption, cronyism and mediocrity that had plagued Haiti for decades.

The administration's attitudes during foreign visits mirrored the same iniquities revealed in its cabinet.

I was behind the scenes on a few foreign trips and understood the dysfunctions and weaknesses of our diplomacy, crowded with unqualified appointees. However, I met some of our best minds in our Foreign Service during those trips—people like Anne Louise Mesadieu and Maguet Delva, whose value represent only a small cog in a wheel meant to promote our interests and values abroad. Our presidents' visits overseas are supposed to follow a long tradition of diplomatic expeditions to demonstrate friendship and cement ties with our allies but, most importantly, to advance our national interests.

In December 2017 we traveled to Paris at a time when the veil of mist and snow already laid over the landscape. I could still see traces of Haiti's abundance in the exuberance of French displays, years of our free labor indirectly sharpening the City of Light. President Emmanuel Macron received President Moïse at the Élysée Palace ahead of the climate change summit to strengthen relations solely based on our shared language, which the majority of Haitians still do not speak. The One Planet Summit was an initiative to engage public and private actors around the world in the race against global warming. The work carried out over the past two years had resulted in a watershed management project in Haiti funded by a mere thirty-million-dollar pledge through the Green Climate

Fund designed to finance commitments made under the Paris Agreement.

The small cohort of press, security, business leaders and aides who surrounded President Moïse followed no carefully designed agenda or guidelines to ensure an efficient trip leading to real negotiations around the creation of active partnerships, networks of exchanges of international cooperation. No significant bilateral accords or trade agreements were signed. The trip was rather a mere photo op that left our trade relations with France still limited.

The intermittent, thunderous applause of our compatriots in the diaspora, hundreds of whom would rally to listen to the president flaunt his accomplishments in campaign style, would restore me. I would always look forward to those moments to mingle with the crowd. "A lot of work is being done without international aid or PetroCaribe funds," he maintained. "We have made tremendous strides in education reform. Ninety percent of children now have access to grade school. Before the end of my term, no child will be left behind." All this a clear depiction of the president's long-stretched imagination, as he continued to make promises despite the magnitude of our challenges, competing priorities and limited resources.

I learned very early in my career that committing to campaign promises is essential to strong leadership.

But the administration failed there too. President Moïse promised to begin the national summit with crucial sectors to find a way of governance that avoided redundant political crises. But he could not. He vowed to make the dreams of pride and greatness that inhabit our people possible by breaking the chains of discord and division. Yet he only worsened the situation. Each presidential commission he created was a theatrical testament of his quest for solutions but only added more financial pressure to the state without ever providing rapid, effective and lasting responses to the problems our country faces.

The fundamental change in the orientation and character of the administration left me disappointed, confused, at a loss for words. If there were a logical way to address my perplexity, one that could provide comfort to me and to the nation, it was never communicated. What I saw was the president promising visions and dreams that were ultimately silenced by the forces of the status quo. Going in, we understood that it would not be easy to change our collective perspective. Past failures, the overcoming of entrenched systems of corruption, the endless struggle that so many had endured, presented us with challenges. However, all around us, Caribbean nations had prospered and grown, overcoming similar problems within failed systems. Why not Haiti?

To follow in their example, the reforms we undertake must always align with the people's will. We need to progress toward a nation no longer isolated, where citizens feel the government is working with them rather than against them. We will encounter resistance from entrenched forces who want only to extract wealth for themselves during the process of any reform. The most significant barrier to a brand-new form of political leadership is the expectation, found throughout society, that nothing can ever change for the better. Our government institutions' natures are far from inclusive; instead, they suffer from a spirit of scheming privilege due to a lack of will to enforce change. A pliant judiciary doesn't help on the odd occasion when laws and regulations are enforced against a corrupt institution. In the end, officials only make things better for themselves.

Breaking from the past takes wisdom. A nation's spirit can develop bad habits, just like a person. If leaders are to prove themselves, influencing the nation's soul into a more positive vibrancy is a worthwhile and prudent effort. As Haitians, we have the good fortune of understanding ourselves. What is necessary is to build reliable institutions that work for the people. That begins with a determination not to get bogged down in the way things are and have always been thinking and get straight to work rebuilding functional institutions that transcend generations. Leadership is key.

Reform is a job we must tackle while accounting for flexibility in our plans and innovation in our approaches. When something works, we must expedite to replicate proven models. Then we must protect and build on what works. When problems occur, we should quickly identify them and double down our efforts, focusing on policy and credible reform promises, including a timeline for enacting changes. Our problems run the risk of getting even worse unless we persistently prioritize the reform goals as we attentively listen to the people.

During my years in the executive office of William A. Flanagan, the mayor of Fall River, I learned that the government must adapt to meet every citizen's needs. A leader must always connect himself to the physical impact of his decisions on the people. I learned that fact in a humbling way when my friend's misstep negatively impacted his team members, his community of supporters and himself.

At the time, a landfill closure forced our administration to implement a highly unpopular pay-as-you-throw program. It became a key element igniting a recall election, a process by which voters can remove an elected official from office through a direct vote before his term has ended. This was an essential scrutiny of the mayor's leadership when the people believed he wasn't properly discharging his responsibilities, an example of democracy at work. Regrettably, Mayor Flanagan lost his seat in that recall election. Looking back on his tenure as a mayor, I extracted much wisdom: a real leader knows that listening to the people is an important part of the job.

Thanks to this wisdom, it became clear to me why I had to leave those meeting rooms of hypotheticals in Haiti in search of a stronger connection to my people. As a government figure—though not of the highest order, a recognizable one—my maturity rising from exposure to the halls of power brought along with it greater moral obligation, a call to duty. Not the glee that comes from a sense of insider knowledge that makes one more powerful than another; I simply became aware that I saw the problem. At the center of decision-making, the interests of the people were not the priority. When entering the administration, I had allowed myself to dream that the well-rehearsed political slogan, "assembling the lands, the sun, the rivers, and the people..." would suffice to advance a better life for our people, bring new vision, as it had a deepening of my optimism. I wanted to work to see the fruition of projects bigger than myself. Instead, I found myself in the roundabouts of amateurism, incompetence and foreign permeation.

My father taught me that there is an urgency within every man to make his mark in the world. Only through the depth of my life experience could I summon the strength to stay true to my principles of a government committed to making life better for others. After twenty-three months as an adviser to President Jovenel Moïse, I resigned in December 2018. And there I was, with the universe turning in such a way as I distanced myself from an administration whose values had become incompatible with my own—without a soft landing, yet it marked the beginning of my making my own imprint on the world.

My colleague Calvin's warning still resonated in my mind, as pounding as the turbulence from our car ride to Artibonite during the presidential campaign. Our conversation gave way to a window into the future. He always believed that my character would not allow me to commit for too long to a public administration. We discussed with passion the real prospects for change in Haiti, and analyzed some of the promises that then-candidate Jovenel Moïse was discussing on the campaign trail. As members of the diaspora, I had expected Calvin not only to believe in but to yearn for a better country. He had lived in foreign lands and relished the luxuries of modernization, the comforts of security, the wages of real patriotism. He had served in the Martelly administration and witnessed the restraints of Haiti's development. I suppose I was looking for realistic reinforcement, an amended balance for my shared optimism with our candidate, when I asked Calvin if he believed the country could change.

But his response had turned our lively conversation somber. As he stared into his phone screen, completing a press release for the campaign, he turned to his left and replied, "If Haiti is to change, it will certainly not be with Jovenel Moïse."

The previous day we had traveled hundreds of miles from Port-au-Prince to Cap-Haitien, then proceeded nonstop to Jérémie to attend campaign rallies, a repetitive exercise that would often leave us drained. With his response came rushing the overwhelming disbelief that some of us could still have reservations even while enduring all the tribulations of the campaign: the hard work, the absence of pay, the sleepless nights, the sacrifices made while being away from loved ones to give our best in support of a candidate's vision to better our homeland. Part of me wanted to remain quiet, while the other part wrestled to keep from screaming, a combination that later amounted to a minor headache.

"Did you mean those words?" I retorted as the other parties in the vehicle laughed at my tenacity.

Calvin calmly expanded, "If you doubt my

statement, Ralf, I guarantee you will not last in our administration."

After those words, I said nothing more.

Calvin later became director of the ministry of communications, a position he'd also held under a previous administration. It still baffles me that many of those who occupy essential roles in our government do not believe in the country. They endlessly imprecate on Haiti and all its leaders as a replacement for mandatory prayers and encouragements appropriate to our heads of state. It should not take a genius to understand this represents an apparent conflict of interest that has transformed the country into a republic of competing priorities. While some public servants do mean well, the era of cynicism that clouded their judgment perpetuated corruption.

✦ ✦ ✦

Following my resignation, the real Haiti, a country on a perilous course, was there to meet me. In recent decades, disasters in the form of earthquakes and hurricanes have had the most devastating impact. Mismanagement has come right alongside recovery efforts, helping to topple trust. Even quantitative evidence of our growth has failed to penetrate the collective consciousness. Our people look upon our history as one of failure, from a personal and an ancestral per-spective. As weak as they are, some fear our institutions will stop functioning altogether unless we continue to allow business as usual. To save face, our leaders help to hide corruption. This method has worked out well for them in the past. When our officials act to supplement their bank accounts with funds and materials that are part and parcel of our institutions' primary functions, those people obstruct the long-sought course toward our founding fathers' dreams.

Instead of seeking a period of contemplation and peace, I used my time away from the administration to turn to my people to listen, learn, grow and steer my ship back to move with its natural current. I met almost every leader of the country's provinces to understand each one's role in Haiti's development. I wanted to offer healing from the divisions in our soci-ety. On my quest, I was reminded of what my good friend Perry used to say: "If you're going to be in ser-vice of others, in relationships with people, you must connect with them, understand them and ultimately work with them; you have to know their story." Perry was as insightful as he was supportive, always pushing me to break out of my comfort zone.

I visited relatives in neighborhoods where hordes of bandits formed accords intended to provide regional peace. I met with many young professionals, college graduates whose academic achievements should have provided their own and national economic growth opportunities, but instead functioned in the informal market. I witnessed many capable young men and women surviving the anguish of unemployment. I gathered in churches with crowds who kept praying and hoping for change while refusing to organize or act in ways that would affect said change. They forgot that it remains a Christian duty to rise against the problems in our country. I met with groups whose rhythmic drums echo, intended to yield goodness in their communities, merely regurgitated the dormant gods into inadvertent malevolence—a conspicuous reality in Haiti, where the majority dismisses them as having a clear influence on the daily lives of the nation. I also discovered many great community leaders: pastors, organizers, teachers, voodoo priests and parents who do not always press forward to take charge of situations. They shrink quietly into the background to inspire, raising generations of good men and women, creating conditions that should motivate their sons and daughters to be productive members of society, move outside their comfort zones and grow beyond their present limitations. Through it all, I learned to put my country first, resist evil and question everything, knowing that eventually, the truth must win in the end.

I would often find myself interrogated and brought before some sort of an impromptu people's court to answer to the wrongdoings my former employer committed against them. It felt as if we were becoming a nation of people who identified ourselves with whom we voted for in the last election. We developed a sneering bitterness toward one another, stopped talking to one another because our politics of conviction diverged, having uncovered one more reason to be divided. People who were drawn to one side would look with disdain on those who were drawn to the other when both sides are necessary for the political system to work. Those who remembered me as a former adviser to the president deemed me guilty by association. It took time to convince some of them otherwise. Having been forced into the defendant's chair, I often argued as if I was right, but always listened as if I was wrong. This combination of listening, conversation and honesty kept their "courtroom" civil. I empathized with those forgotten few who had lost faith in the ways of government; they were tired and worn down. They were out of patience for the intolerable and dreadful destitution that left their children to starve, their neighbors to occasionally riot, their young friends to flee the country and their cousins to live jobless in large communes. However, the silent majority, with shared optimism, continued to help Haitians steer through daily unresolved issues, fighting for a better country for all, yearning for a newer form of leadership that protects, promotes and provides hope.

In their respective way, both of my parents engaged in the fight for a better Haiti, all the while preparing me for my journey ahead. My mother, a nurse, inspired my capacity for hope. Through her, I witnessed its essence, watching as the front porch of my childhood home in Valère filled up and overflowed with patients from all over the region. Some appeared with ailments she was able to treat immediately. Many more had chronic conditions that needed ongoing treatment. Still others would return with smiles on their faces and words of gratitude, bearing small gifts and thank-you notes. Mom healed the wounded, diagnosed the sick, brought out sheer bliss and reassured with hope for the future in all her patients for little or no money. She instilled in me a sizable appreciation for the human experience and a discernible ability to practice compassion.

On the other hand, my father taught me leadership principles: integrity, strength, wisdom, prudence and virtue from the church's pulpit. As a pastor and advocate for social change, he volunteered his time and financial resources to make our town a better place. Dad believed that community building was a fluid process. Once he migrated to the United States, his leadership continued to transcend our homeland to impact the diaspora. At the same time, he taught me to cultivate high social and religious aspirations through often rigorous methods. Failure to attend church activities was frowned upon and subjected to corporal punishment. Over time, I learned to link self-respect with prayer, patience and persistence.

Growing up in the church inspired me to adhere to an unwavering optimism in life. There, I also learned the importance of truth and courage, as well as the meaning of community. I would often call on that faith to endure the stress of public service, and to escape the boundaries of oppression that had been set for my generation. In a defining experience in my pursuit of understanding Haiti, I met a brilliant spiritual scholar named McManaway. He and I talked about the spiritual heritage of our politics of cynicism, the moral degradation in our leadership and some of the solutions to overcome. He became a mentor and a friend and was convinced that my energetic personality and record of achievements promised bright prospects to advance me beyond my peers. He was cognizant that this would be both a blessing and a challenge; it is as easy for a person to feel threatened by my considerable optimism as it is for them to admire it.

Thanks to my parents, I remained firm in my desire to invest my all for the greater good. They helped me realize that to make a difference, to be the difference in someone else's life, is a requirement of good citizenry. Thus, leadership begins at home. This is why when parents raise their children to be good citizens, they take part in building a better Haiti.

✦ ✦ ✦

Our evolution in leadership should transcend governmental and societal patterns. It needs to involve the political parties and business leaderships to focus all efforts on promoting political stability and the rule of law.

During my past years living in Haiti, I realized the idea of a political opposition is simply a farce. In truth, there is the government and the private sector, and each camp has its mercenaries. The use of the word "mercenaries" is not at all an overstatement. They are otherwise known as those agents of destruction who have no vested interests, other than gaining monetary advantages, in Haiti's development. The relationship between the government and the contentious economic establishment remains an unresolved issue marked by constant

Our evolution in leadership should transcend governmental and societal patterns

tension. The political manipulation of this relationship has had profound consequences for the country for decades. They fight, tear each other apart, unite and conspire to satisfy their interests—and the people, taken hostage, continue to suffer.

One of the recent illustrations of conflict between the government and the private sector has been over the power supply in Haiti. Energy has long been a persistent issue. Of the nine million people in the Caribbean who lack electricity, more than seven live in Haiti. Limited access to affordable and consistent power obstructs investments, constrains development and degrades citizens' living standards. One of the priorities laid out in the interim government plan in March 2004 was reestablishing continuous electrical service. Years later, the electricity sector still faces crucial problems: lack of financial and human resources for maintenance, fragmentation of the main actors, poor management practices, continued political interference, fraud and corruption, weak capacity of the institutional framework and the lack of strategic coordination and leadership.

President Moïse refused to preside over a country wracked by chronic energy shortages. He made reform a top priority, promising to make constant electricity available in the entire country in two years from July 2017. The president's objective raced ahead, with several different permutations of what the solutions to Haiti's electricity crisis should be. He became the fourth president to undertake critical reforms in the electricity sector. In relieving all renewable energy and energy efficiency equipment from import duties the administration made great strides toward mapping a new course for the country's electricity sector. Many experts suggested that the power problem would take several presidential terms to resolve, even in a climate of political stability. The blend of a culture of nonpayment for electrical services, relatively high consumption rates, a low base of metered customers, a lack of support from the authorities to combat corruption and fraud and widespread electricity theft were the established reasons for the crumbling electrical network and significant financial losses.

Instead of helping to reform the electricity sector into effective, financially healthy companies that provide continuous and reliable power to the entire country, the president's steadfast determination provoked the reactions of the business leaders' ruling oligarchy. There was a long list of political discourse, propaganda and legal disputes feeding their anger, thereby worsening the crisis. Some of the key electricity providers were determined to obstruct all reforms not made by or with them. Moreover, public opinion was divided between those who deemed the government's electricity reform legitimate and others who saw only a president's political agenda.

The divide was so deep, it was almost as if the manipulative propaganda machines were winning the war on truth. Haiti was facing a crisis of confidence, was a country being sold to the highest bidder. The special-interest groups who wished to overthrow the government financed a full-scale assault on our democracy. They became such experts at manipulating the truth that many from my generation continued to absorb their devious narratives and fake news with phenomenal ease. Therefore, we must remain vigilant regarding the facts if we genuinely want to rebuild a better country; there should always be an openness to finding possible other sides of the stories we hear. We must judge our collective progress by the tenacity in our questions, the honesty in our answers, our inclination to embrace truth in lieu of what feels right.

We must look beyond the theatrical display of charming words, the false antipoverty prophets, the power-hungry individuals, continually reminding ourselves of the facts. Haiti already has most of the key building blocks necessary to achieve substantial energy reform—with important exceptions on the legal front. The energy crisis that persists is due to a leadership deficit. Business leaders and government officials continue to fail Haiti and its citizens while they abuse the public trust to serve their own interests. Our economic crisis is the direct result of the politically unstable environment they foster to discourage world financial backers' support and a subsequent lack of interest from international donors in our sustainable development initiatives.

✦ ✦ ✦

Political stability is imperative for Haiti's economic growth, just as a stable sociopolitical environment helps build a coherent and continuous path for sustainable development. Stability, however, is not a stagnant concept. No society or social system can function in a completely stable environment except in a utopia. Every political and social system undergoes some periods of instability and disorganization. But in the case of Haiti, it is chronic. Achieving the goal of overall stability has been a challenge for every administration. Each one assumes that the prospect of our political and social stability will depend merely on how they absorb various groups into the public administration and the political system. Each promotes a culture of cohabitation by giving senior-level positions to political parties and social groups in opposition to facilitating stability. This tradition has turned our government into the largest employer and rendered politics as the first national economy.

Cohabitation has not worked. The diverse beliefs of all the political parties and influencers from different social groups only invigorated the frequent change of government personnel, another formula of instability that negatively impacts the national economy. In 2018, when President Moïse planned to nominate Jean-Henry Céant, a member of the opposition, to be his prime minister, I cautioned that it was a dangerous venture. I had my reservations on whether such an alliance regime could yield positive results for Haiti. In my mind, no one could prevent the inevitable: a direct conflict of interest that would result in a power grab. I was not the only one who held that sentiment.

"Mr. President," Emmanuel, the communication director, uttered in a low, deep voice from the corner of the room, "I am with Ralf on this one," thereby reinforcing my reservations.

Emmanuel, an adviser to the president, was one of the administration's sound minds. He did not believe the new prime minister would be a conciliatory figure to reach across the aisle to speak with all actors to remove political blockages.

Céant was a rival presidential candidate in 2016, a political party leader who advocated for different solutions from President Moïse on many important policy issues. The president thought it was smart to choose those with opposing viewpoints, that they would add value to his political agenda and obtain results for Haiti. But Céant's nomination only led to further erosion of the president's authority through frequent disagreements.

I witnessed some of the conflicts, the first wave of which was over the appointment of ministers. There was a huge contrast between Céant and his predecessor. With Jack Guy Lafontant as prime minister, the president was in control; every decision went through him. Céant's appointment shifted the power structure, leading many political actors to gather in his office to align themselves. Political realignment is the culture in Haiti, though rarely this early in a presidential term; at that point, Moïse had been in office for less than two years. This sort of growing disinterest in an administration usually happens in the last year of a presidential term. But Céant knew how to play the game well; he was actively pulling forces from the private sector, political parties, and special-interest groups to strengthen his base.

Shortly after Céant's appointment, the National Palace felt empty. Everyone could sense the power shift. We would regroup in the "Apartment" during tough times, a one-story lodge situated on the National Palace's southeast lawn, with a tasteful and modern design, built for the president's convenience after the earthquake. It became our sanctuary. There, sitting at the round kitchen table, we debated and proposed solutions to the many pressing issues facing the country. We called ourselves the Disciples, the bunch most loyal to the president. Having been part of the campaign, we had lived through tough days before; power shifts were nothing new. We were considered the opposition during Privert's interim administration and knew all too well what it felt like to be in one camp or the other.

At times, the president would join us in the Apartment. His presence would not change the passion in our voices during our lively debates. It was an opportunity for him to let down his guard; we were like family. I was mostly the quiet one whenever he visited. I wanted to maintain a balance between professionalism and camaraderie. Nonetheless, I always spoke my mind with much directness when required. My colleague and friend Christine often thought my candor was refreshing. Others misinterpreted it for arrogance. But no one's bluntness compared to Nancy's.

"President, I don't like the direction of all this," she would state in a worried tone as the president stirred sugar in his coffee. "Everyone is rallying around Céant."

As the president's facial expression revealed his

burdens, he would shrug and softly say, "We can only wish them luck." As I came to understand it later, that statement was a quantum leap in belligerence toward Prime Minister Céant.

It was clear that the prime minister took advantage of the president's disapproval to perpetrate a coup d'état. Days after his confirmation before Parliament, intelligence reports placed his close advisers in meetings with members of radical groups encouraging protests. Close advisers from the primature were starting to call him "His Excellency." The prime minister forgot the tasks he was nominated to do. Since he became prime minister, the country's condition had worsened. The measures he took to reduce the cost of living and government spending were unsuccessful. The minefield of the people's frustration remained vast during the economic emergency.

The president publicly voiced his dissatisfaction with Prime Minister Céant. Everyone who had been following the infighting understood the move as a calculated one to decelerate Céant's power grab. In response, the prime minister vowed to deepen the investigation into alleged corruption in the PetroCaribe oil program. That was the president's weak spot. His name was at the center of a six-hundred-page report stating that he had allegedly embezzled funds from a PetroCaribe road repair project before he came to office, while he served as head of his own company, Agritrans.

It is not enough to simply conduct an investigation and generate a report. Too many of the proponents of a PetroCaribe trial lack the moral authority to oversee such a critical case. My generation, and future ones as well, have been victims of a massive deception. We need a forensic audit to determine the where, when, how, and who as it pertains to PetroCaribe's funds. Subsequently, the forensic audit results will allow the government to take into account the conclusions and recommendations. Any action taken should be based on evidence, not on suspicion or speculation. Justice must hold accountable anyone who has misused funds with the strictest application of the law.

In his own defense, the president denied any guilt and vowed to bring to justice anyone responsible through a fair, equitable trial without political persecution. Because of the PetroCaribe divergence, the tension between the president and the prime minister escalated so quickly that their promises to work together blew up precisely six months later in a messy parliamentary no-confidence vote orchestrated by the presidency. Sadly, Haiti lurches from one political crisis to another, and the ultimate causes of these instabilities are ultimately rooted in the ignorance, the greed and the thirst for power of our leaders.

As it appeared, there was a celebratory dance in the National Palace after Céant's termination. Elected officials, supporters of the president and cabinet members stopped by to bow before His Excellency for vanquishing the enemy. It was politics as usual. A few feet away from the festive nonsense, in Champs de Mars, there were still constant reminders of the poverty, food insecurity and unemployment those leaders should have been working to eradicate. Haiti was once again the casualty of its leaders' ambitions for power.

The morning following Céant's termination, I pondered our former presidents' relative silence in times of crisis. It was almost as if they had deserted their people, fading in the hidden pile of history consorting with our many curses. In William Shakespeare's *King Henry IV, Part I*, he cautioned against life's fragility and the humility consumed in death: "…ill-weaved ambition, how much art thou shrunk! When that this body did contain a spirit, a kingdom for it was too small a bound; But now two paces of the vilest earth is room enough." I keep praying that our former presidents are preserved from the dangers of riches and the horrors of poverty, that they be kept in an honest humility lest both extremes upset their hearts. If only they understood the height of their responsibilities to liberty, equality and fraternity, they would have cultivated modesty and prudence to fulfill those duties faithfully. They would rid themselves of vainglorious ambitions and profited from their limited time on earth to leave behind legacies worthy of a greater Haiti.

In other nations, former presidents have a unique ability, exceptional platforms to unify their country in crises. Sometimes they are called upon to play the roles of moral politicians, party strengtheners and vocal leaders of the partisan opposition, just as they maintained the presidential office's institutional prestige. Haiti needs the network of its former presidents, prime ministers and other leaders brought together by the desire to build a better country, a leadership that yields political stability to uphold the dignity of the republic.

I had already left the administration before the clash between the president and Prime Minister Céant intensified. That did not stop me from feeling some anger at the narrowness in the president's views. During his episode with the prime minister, the wall separating him from everyone else grew higher, the confining bubble larger. He trusted no one and listened only to himself. He treated those who lingered in his circle, including the Disciples, with contempt and deceit, a stain of mental slavery that still obstructs our human evolution. He turned the presidency into his island: small, independent from the rest of the country, suppressing the voices of the already marginalized.

Too many times, my friend Naikema would complain about this. She was afraid that the president kept himself too secluded and was becoming out of touch. And she was right. I saw it as a conscious choice because he made no effort to change. In many ways, he preferred living in an echo chamber of a few idolizers who only praised his commands, a circle of advisers working to dull the impact of his poor decisions. Remaining in that bubble, he forgot that the growing anger and frustration during his presidency was more pressing than any fleeting pleasure Céant's removal could provide. The fact remained, the people were still out there in protest, fighting to make their voices heard. They had legitimate concerns that needed to be addressed.

Haiti was rapidly becoming a dystopia; free speech was under attack. The police used excessive force to disassemble peaceful protests and target journalists covering public events. The economy was teetering on the edge of collapse. As international aid declined, the government turned to the Banque de la Republic d'Haiti, the Central Bank, to manage the economy. By the summer of 2018, Haiti was facing rising inflation, a growing budget deficit, currency devaluations, a worsening in the preponderance of gang violence. We were on the verge of revolution. But the president dismissed the collective voice. To appease the political climate, the president reshuffled his cabinet to give jobs to key leaders from the opposition. The vicious cycle was in full swing. The people's anger emerged full force into an era of political instability that paralyzed the country for several months.

Such chaos was beneficial to President Moïse regardless of how many private properties were damaged or lives lost. The anarchy, protests and violence that erupted across the country provided him with the excuse he needed to postulate a tough-guy argument and blame the political opposition for enabling criminal behaviors. It was almost as if politics had replaced his human compassion and wisdom. The chaos was a real test of our resolve as a nation, a time for us to put politics aside and begin a dialogue to inspire change. The forces that can trigger alterations will come from listening to one another. It was a time for us to come together to decide which country we sought to leave behind for future generations. Conversely, neither the administration nor the political opposition chose to put Haiti first; they carried on an incessant fight to gauge the strongest camp to remain standing.

A colleague once said to me about politics in

Haiti, "Ralf, just like we learned it in school, 'might is right,'" in a firm tone, clenching his left fist as a symbol of despotism. During the campaign, Jovenel Moïse emphasized much of this philosophy in this statement: "We are more, we are stronger, wiser, and we will not back down." Political leaders typified this so many times that it became a feature of our national character.

I once heard an aspiring leader of my generation addressing a crowd of promising young adults. He enumerated only three choices for their future prospects: leave the country, stay to die or stand up and fight. In essence, his statement was an echo of Jean de La Fontaine's logic, the idea that my generation was stronger united in the face of flagrant hopelessness. I could not be sure if the leader's radical thoughts came out of pure manipulation, or had he already been, without realizing it, the product of the same environment he was criticizing. We are too quick to advance force and resilience as substitutes for reason and common sense.

I learned the power of words at an early age. Words create, motivate and empower, but they also destroy. In the *Educator's Book,* Sigmund Freud talked about how our words can significantly impact our lives and the lives of others. They can help, heal, harm or humiliate. My father used to stress that the choices we make in our language define our character. He cautioned me never to speak without contemplating the immense force that flows from my speech. "A carefully curated sermon is worth a thousand weapons," Dad would say. He was right; words are truly invisible weapons. They can move people, shaping the destiny of an entire nation.

The moral lesson of de La Fontaine is not absolute truth; it is often a principal danger. The story of David and Goliath provides caution and wisdom. Of course, I am not suggesting that we retreat from activism. Haiti needs all its sons and daughters to have a voice during its reconstruction. But the culture of revolt and the overthrowing of every leadership has not borne fruit. By tearing one another apart for so long, we believed that our country's socioeconomic development was above human capacity. Beware of leaders who politicize our concerns, employ aggressive words to encourage us to be brave, to fight the system. There exist shrewder ways to resist the conditions of our underdevelopment. There is no room for another revolution.

What Haiti needs is *evolution*. We must begin with an attitude, an outlook mixed with unrestrained political enthusiasm, a grassroots movement to reconnect our youth with politics, fix the broken system, reshape our country's direction.

Haiti needs new perspectives on its old problem of

instability. Our leaders must look at its questions from a standpoint that ensures development, freedom and harmony. Instead of cohabitating, they should aim to provide legitimacy to the needs and demands of social groups and classes, particularly the most vulnerable sections of the population.

Scholars in the field have done a thorough job of identifying the most popular political stability measures: the absence of civil unrest or violence, acceptance of political legitimacy, effective decision-making, persistence of patterns and authenticity of democratic structures.[*]

Haiti needs new perspectives on its old problem of instability

Given our present sociopolitical reality, our government officials, politicians and business leaders must agree on fulfilling these critical elements to achieve stability and prosperity in Haiti. The good news is that among my generation, there is a considerable yearning, an enormous dedication to rebuilding a better country, a newer system that works for everyone. It, however, is not likely to come about without struggles. We must start by eliminating political violence as an industry. Many Haitians have identified this as one of our most significant obstacles to stability; it is a multimillion-dollar business in our country. No one can be elected without using the service, directly or indirectly. Inside the disenfranchised pockets of major cities, ongoing recruitment to participate in protests-for-money has replaced job-skills training and career fairs, and election time is peak recruitment season. Candidates who wish to organize marches and rallies to reinforce the perception of popularity must pay-for-play. Many people, encountering trouble with the basic necessities, bury their moral objections and become adept at uprisings: barricading streets, burning tires and destroying private properties for an expert-level service fee, missions usually imposed by a dangerous network of unknowns.

The reek of this system speaks of two failures: a miscarriage of economic justice and a grave failure to provide recourse for social frustrations. Unfortunately, the police force has been infiltrated. Gangs and politicians alike are influencing the population, whose anger and disappointment are easily manipulated. Over the last thirty years, mass resentment has destroyed our society's moral fabric, replacing ambition with envy and tolerance with hatred. The target of that rage has always been elected officials and the wealthy.

We must lean toward reform. The Haitian government must guarantee a peaceful, law-abiding society, devoid of politically motivated violent behaviors to influence decisions. We must collectively accept that change results from established procedures, not an unethical process that solves issues through conflict and aggression.* In the words of Harry H. Eckstein, "Stable democracy requires a congruence of authority patterns between government and segments of social life that resist democratization, it requires balances of contradictory behavior patterns, in such a way that the balances do not lead to undue strain and intolerable anomie; it requires a certain similarity among authority patterns, but not to the extent that basic human need is thwarted."†

Political legitimacy is also a vital component of stability. It begins with free, fair and transparent elections. But officials, once elected, need to beware that no authority is absolute. They must continuously work to secure the consent of the people when making decisions. Inherent in every democracy is the natural right to revolt. It is not an extended license to overthrow governments for any given reason. Because men's nature can be chaotic when there is no authority to restrain individual will, the government becomes a necessity to maintain stability. But when cold, rational reason dictates that the current condition is a threat to the country's continued existence, the people must and should act.

Just as much, the government requires the governed to remain legitimate. Legitimacy is not only the absence of strong dissent but the presence of acceptance and support from the people. Therefore, when a government oversteps the boundaries of natural law, it ceases to be legitimate. The perspectives of political philosophers John Locke and Thomas Hobbes on this matter were fundamental in our founding fathers' strongest justifications for independence. Furthermore, our most recent democratic reforms still incorporate the notion of consent, central to the Lockean political theory, as the ideal of a government for the people and by the people.*

Thus, our leaders must continuously summon their courage to question what is morally wrong or right for our country if we want our children to thrive in a tolerant republic, an inclusive Haiti of constant self-recreation through effective decision-making. It is the third principle through which we can reach stability. The bedrock moral requirement for our leaders should be honesty. The question they must ask themselves when making decisions is what is in it for the people? Narrating a policy problem and finding the appropriate solution to adopt is not an easy task. It is, in fact, political. It is the reason debates among political actors to impose their take on a problem seem endless. I often talked to the president about the need for a public policy research institute in Haiti: a place where scholars, organizations, scientists and policymakers can work together with stakeholders to make effective decisions. Science can allow us to overrule our cultural and primitive intuitions to prevent making mistakes. Crafting public policy through legislation is a topic in which expertise should outweigh popular argument. I passionately believe this scientific approach of informing policy through data is a crucial complement to the principles of democracy and the rule of law we urgently require as a nation.

Our political stability will also be illustrated in the persistence of patterns because government longevity or endurance reflects a stable environment that inspires progress. The lack of continuity of government is a serious problem to overcome in Haiti. It squelches our ability to create long-term prosperity through development that must continue over several administrations. The building of a highway system, and the concomitant building of infrastructure that goes with it, cannot happen in just a few years.

In my lifetime alone, Haiti has seen fifteen presidents. That means, on average, each presidency has lasted only two and a half years. The constitutionally acceptable number of presidents, to hold office for five years, should have been eight. Our political culture of factionalism, the pulls and pressures from the private sector, the complexity of options perpetuated by politicians with different ideologies result in all stakeholders asking one frequent and discouraging question: Should any government last? As a result, a widespread universal conception has developed within the masses, holding that no government could ever be good.

Although it is difficult to maintain stability in a multiparty regime such as in our country, many political theorists argue that it is not impossible, provided the democratic regime is "consociational" in character. In a consociational democracy, we base power-sharing on the cooperative attitude of the elites and leaders of different segments of the population.*

Some of Haiti's elites are already powerful within the system. They have a vital role in shaping sociopolitical and -economic policies. These are things that have been true about the elites for as long as I can remember. The owners and controllers of major business enterprises, television and radio stations, legislators and ministers and editors of major newspapers comprise the first tier of this influential group. They also encompass the lower level to include prominent intellectuals, lawyers and doctors, heads of large universities, leaders of religious establishments and real estate developers. The elites' protectiveness of themselves and their status makes for a very hermetic social group; they do business, bank and socialize only among themselves.

However, their rhetorical and political commitment

to development has come under increased scrutiny recently. President Moïse has claimed that they were corrupt and predatory oligarchs who sought to monopolize all areas of development. My generation has accused them of being irresponsible and unconcerned with the modernization and development of Haiti. Our history supports these claims. When compared with elites from other developing nations, their relative development performance is shameful.

Yet the country's current condition poses a threat to them just as much as to the rest of us regarding social and political unrest. First, we, as a people, must be mindful of that fact. Then we can achieve a successful cooperative attitude among both the elites and the leaders of other segments of the population. Development should not be the priority mission and target of government alone. Public actions to promote better leadership and economic growth should be the elites' primary agenda because they too stand to gain even more than they are experiencing now. Then we can achieve successful cooperation between the elites and leaders of different segments of the population.

Moreover, there is an undisputable responsibility that comes with elite status. In other developing nations, the elites play a crucial role in education, health care, technological innovation through philanthropy, civic engagements and political activism. We are not too far from a consociational democracy in Haiti. Perhaps it is a lack of clarity in planning that obstructs productive cooperation between political leaders, elite members and actors across sectors to protect, promote and provide for the country and its people.

If we are to foster political stability, our public institutions must never be mere facades for nondemocratic structures. We must respect their authenticity, modernize and reinforce them to curb corruption, support our foreign policy initiatives and deliver the services Haitians deserve in the most efficient manner possible.

I mentioned conflict of interest as one of the reasons political cohabitation has not worked. But another reason is that in its practice, many of our state institutions become instruments to major corruptive forces, compromising our government's integrity and reducing public trust. Too often do our leaders undermine and insult the integrity of our institutions. Under Interim President Privert, circumventing the rule of law was rampant. Upon taking office, he immediately called for a commission to investigate the elections. The commission alleged that massive fraud had taken place and recommended throwing out the election results. He also fired hundreds of civil servants and replaced them with his partisans and elected officials' paramours and relatives. He had no mandate to do any of these things. His brazen behaviors were proof he had no plans to leave office in 120 days, as required by the February 5th Accord. He publicly defied a senate resolution ordering him to vacate the presidency, brushing aside the Constitution to remain president for a year. His extended stay later raised the most controversial constitutional question around the current presidential term expiration, nourishing political uncertainty.

The Senate later recanted its position against Interim President Privert, citing an administrative blunder. It was claimed that the document signed by the Senate president required the institution's stamp to be valid. Who would have thought! For a moment, it felt as if that episode was whittling away whatever was left of my dream that Haiti could move forward from its many fundamental problems. It was during a presidential campaign when debates also were centered around strengthening our institutions. At that time, a novice in Haitian politics, I was left with many questions. Instead of reneging, why couldn't the Senate add the stamp to the document to authenticate it? If strong institutions are considered essential for our growth, why do our politicians continue to instrumentalize them to their needs?

The people of Haiti were not asking for any special

favors. The country simply deserved an elected president and not a provisional government selected by the traditional political elites that continued to subvert the democratic principles we hold dear. If I learned one thing from American politics, it was that it takes one simple offense to take a public servant down; a crime is almost impossible to survive. In Haiti, we often reward acts of misconduct with pats on the back, all to the country's detriment. The alarming number of self-interested and unethical public servants has created a comfortable network that reduces our institutions almost to nothingness.

Sometimes, our leaders weaken our institutions without realizing it. I remember President Moïse's famous speech of September 4, 2017, marking the start of the school year. He spoke passionately against corruption, emphasizing it five times as the problem hindering our progress. He was right; corruption is widespread in the country, as are allegations of the impunity that undermines the foundation of the rule of law and incites practices that jeopardize peace, security and political stability. In an anecdote, he complained that he was forced to nominate corrupt judges based on submission by the judicial council tasked with vetting nominees. That was a strong assault undermining yet another branch of government.

The independence of the judiciary branch warrants no compromise from any president. When fueled by politics and corruption, the way we choose our judges can undermine the public's faith in impartial justice. The president's statement failed to promote an independent, competent and ethical judiciary. It contributed to the decades of dysfunction in our judicial system, perpetuating the lack of faith in our democracy. There is no sustainable democracy without justice. Thus, the rule of law is essential to stability. Combining the absence of civil unrest, the acceptance of political legitimacy, the new principle for effective decision-making and the respect for our democratic institutions' authenticity, it can culminate in long-lasting governments that will drive several generations to achieve their dream of boundless realities for Haiti.

✦ ✦ ✦

The abundance of parties in our political culture contributes to the inconsistencies in our political system. Since 1987, we have organized fifteen elections, every single one a source of conflict. When a candidate loses, he points to irregularities, brings fraud allegations or starts an uprising. Usually, the governments' response to those post-election protests is repression, which only makes matters worse. The people eventually lose faith. Only 21 percent of registered voters cast a ballot in the last presidential election. Before we may hold honest dialogues about securing better elections, we must agree to reduce Haiti's number of political parties.

In 2014, just before my return, the number of members required to form a political party was reduced from five hundred to twenty, leading to the creation of numerous political parties—most of them small—aggregating and articulating different interests. Instead of bringing together a vibrant number of people with similar political convictions that add value to the political dialogue in the periods between elections, we have a phoenixlike system that rises from the ashes before an election and burns itself up after the process.

Many political parties exist merely as fronts for ambitious individuals, or vehicles to advance one politician's agenda. None of the current parties are structured with loyal members. Leaders tend to change parties as they please, and they do not support any public policy issues or a well-developed program. Like the national government, political parties have been unsuccessful in addressing the needs of the vast majority of Haitians who live outside the capital and other urban areas. Their objective has been more to field candidates in local and national elections, not to connect the people with their government.

As I examined the results of presidential elections since the inception of democracy in Haiti, it became apparent that the statistics repudiate our culture of having too many presidential candidates. In any number of elections, the top three or four candidates always retain 80 percent of the votes. It is hard for any other candidates to secure more than 5 percent of the vote individually.

In contrast, in the United States, primaries are held to purge the pool of candidates before general elections. Many of the leaders spend years working their way up the political ladder. Some of them start their careers in leadership positions in the youth organizations of their parties, which allow them to rise to regional or national political leadership. Others begin their journey by running for local office and working their way up through the ranks.

I began my own political journey at the local level as an active member of the Democratic Party in the United States. In those years, the New Bedford city committee suffered from the same illnesses of decreased public participation as most other local party structures. I had a chance to work with many distinguished individuals and to learn from their experience, among them Marlene Pollock, whose voice keeps repeating in my head with her notions of history and activism that informed my ideals. That is where I met my good friends and political operatives extraordinaire, Dana Rebeiro and Lisa Lemieux. We became inseparable, the new blood in town, organizing strategies to revive the local party.

The issues affecting our part of Massachusetts were continually evolving, and dialogue between the local citizens and candidates running for public office was needed more than ever. Dana, Lisa and I, with the help of the ever-able MarDee Xifaras, collaborated with other Democratic city and town committees, local organizations and stakeholders throughout the South Coast to highlight issues on transportation, public safety, education, the economy and the environment, to organize a Democratic gubernatorial candidates forum.

It was an exciting chance for New Bedford residents to hear directly from those who wished to govern the state. More importantly, it secured an occasion for these candidates to hear from citizens about the region's most critical issues. There is a catchphrase in American political culture: All politics is local. Ultimately, people vote according to the concerns and issues that affect their personal lives and hometowns. All five Democratic candidates of the time attended the forum. That year's Democratic primary was filled with highly qualified candidates, proposing bold, innovative ideas and ambitious goals. We brought the gubernatorial campaign to New Bedford with the hope that everyone would walk away more informed. It is one of the rights the Democratic Party ensures in the United States. It is the kind of political landscape I wish for Haiti.

In many other countries, the political system is also organized and stabilized around two or three significant poles facilitating voters' choice. We too can establish a democratic political system based on poles of ideas for the country's benefit. We need bold leadership to reform the political landscape. In this spirit, during my days as an adviser to the president, I proposed a three-party-platform system to mitigate inconsistencies during presidential elections. I was hopeful when the president met with political party leaders and representatives to initiate reform of the provisions relating to public funding in the 2014 Political Parties Act. I saw it as an opportunity to end the cycle of chaos and set a course on a sustainable, peacefully engaging political landscape.

I often reflect on the president's response to my proposition. He uttered words that left me with a hurtful memory. "Ralf," he said in a delicate tone, as he looked to the floor and crossed his left leg over the right. His comfort was unchecked, sitting on that presidential chair from the Duvalier era. "The problem is never that your suggestions are not upright and worthy." And then he added, "Your mind is not formatted for Haiti."

It is not as if I did not expect there would be obstacles to implementing a three-party-platform system. In Haiti, democracy is accepted only in theory—a minority of the players behave according to democratic principles. For instance, the ruling class's main objective is to remain in power and make money, while those not in power seek access to high-profile government positions for financial gain. Thus, I was confident that such an initiative would be worthwhile for our country's democratic health and sustainability.

The president's words left me perplexed. He could spot the disappointment in my expression and quickly continued: "This system would only work in other countries. Haitian politicians would never agree." At that point, I was not sure whether his last words were meant to appease my bewilderment or to provide a broader context for the complexities surrounding my proposal.

Naikema was in the room that day. We had developed a silent signal to keep each other in check in moments of disappointment. She lightly scratched her neck as she looked away to signal her stupefaction. Still, today, I cannot fathom how our leaders could remain so intolerant and contemptuous in the face of the hard choices they ought to make for Haiti. They continuously push them aside for the next generation of leaders to deal with. They only act when divisive issues are groundbreaking reasons for uprisings and the political unrest that can disrupt their terms in office.

Later, I learned that the president's statement was a compliment. The reforms I proposed, more robust party platforms, challenged the status quo, providing a stronger legal framework for legitimacy, and not just during elections. Because party platforms are created by compromise and consensus, they can address the lack of trust between political parties and the Commission Electorale Provisoire (CEP). I have seen parties come and go in the past years, and the legislature's functioning suffers. Individual members become more apt to act in their own self-interest. But when parties adhere to platforms and have an ongoing, functioning internal power structure, it can be easier to discipline within the ranks. The leaders would be less authoritarian than the ones we have now. Ideas become essential, not so much the person in leadership. There exist parameters for changing leadership and a base within the system that can merge behind an alternative that does not seek to throw the country into chaos because they lost an election.

This party-platform system is nothing new to our politics. It involves smaller political parties coming together to form a coalition, giving individual members a certain prestige in the country's political life and encouraging citizens' participation in our democratic process on an ongoing basis. When a teacher or farmer can reach out to local leadership with their issues, and those leaders are responsive to their concerns, that is inclusive democracy and effective governance, allowing candidates and parties to reach out to voters and to build long-term political organizations.

Unregulated or poorly managed money in politics is one of the biggest threats to democracy worldwide. In a country like Haiti, it has led incumbent politicians and political parties to abuse state resources to maintain a dominant party system whose defeat becomes unlikely for the foreseeable future. Such abuse of state resources by the ruling party, putting itself in an advantageous position, creates an unfair playing field that undermines our electoral integrity. The international community increasingly recognizes that such corruption and abuse remain the most significant problem in reforming Haiti's broken political system, prohibiting the equal participation and representation of all citizens in democratic political processes. Unregulated money in politics has also led our politicians to listen to their sponsors rather than their voters. Often sizable government contracts are awarded to the company that provided the most funds during the last campaign rather than the one with the best bid.

The party-platform structure can provide better transparency on how much money flows in elections, the funds' sources and how they are spent. It can curb corruption and promote citizens' trust in political institutions. A party-platform structure can efficiently fix the quota mandate for women in the political system's decision-making bodies. I met more women leaders and candidates in party-platform political structures in Haiti, establishing an inclusive electoral process that allows for healthy, even loud, debate. Suppose we must continue to work to strengthen our democracy. We need to promote debate, but without fostering the kind of environment that sees tires burning in the street, destroying property and harming those on all sides of an election or other contested issue. Improvements in the party and election system will encourage a mature political class with stronger ethical standards that act as barriers against corruption. There is a difference between party platform as a structure and the political system in which it operates. While some existing party platforms may bear the burden of a political actor's corrupt action, the merit of the structure and its ability to streamline the electoral process should not be questioned.

EMPOWERMENT

*A prosperous Haiti with a legacy of strong citizens,
effective government and ethical business traditions—
a country in which we can all succeed if we try.*

HAITI IS NOT open for business. Anyone who proclaims otherwise is devious and likely saying so for personal gain. Without spending very much time in the country, one quickly discerns the truth. The business environment has not improved. The country continues to break records for low classifications of doing business in reports published by international institutions. The embassies of the countries that call themselves our allies continue to advise their nationals against doing business in Haiti. The current state of our social dynamics motivates too many unethical and criminal behaviors at all levels of our society; there is almost no honest, lawful way to prosperity. The path to wealth forks in two directions: immoral or illegal. Our people learn entrepreneurship as a way of getting by—a "survival-skill," free-enterprise model that lacks options for a long-term focus and a vision for growth. And that type of business pursuit leads to behaviors that play no collectively important role.

Years after the earthquake, we are still struggling to solve our country's most pressing problems. Even before that natural disaster, the government struggled to guarantee the rule of law, deliver a legal framework of rights and implement strategies that allow citizens and businesses to freely exercise those rights. The lack of coordination of resources and capacity thwarted public service developments, social programs, efficient transportation networks, public education systems, critical infrastructure—all the enabling conditions required for citizens' empowerment to contribute to building a sustainable economy.

Moreover, the maze many of us must navigate to meet our daily needs leaves little time to participate in the rebuilding of the sociopolitical system. Economic conditions are precarious. The lack of a reliable legal system and access to credit, property ownership issues, political corruption and primary infrastructure problems such as access to clean water and electricity continue to hamper development.

In response, most Haitians have established their own small subsistence economies, resorting to home-based businesses such as stores, small manufacture and retail spaces. Because of this, the country has remained dependent on international economic assistance to make its fiscal obligations sustainable, with foreign aid and direct budget support accounting for 20 percent of the nation's annual budget.

The state of affairs in Haiti must change. A country's economic health is in direct correlation to how empowered its citizens are. The ability to end economic stagnation rests on our business leaders' ability to start and manage sustainable enterprises that fulfill more than momentary needs. Their business models must include corporate responsibility; in other words, in doing business, they should also strive to serve. This would require our government to lower barriers and create a sustainable system of access to capital, licensure and property rights, so people can form companies they open with the confidence that they will operate them unimpeded and with a sense of moral responsibility to their country.

Processes never go as expected when opening a business in Haiti. Start-ups must navigate an impossible bureaucracy. No matter how expert one's planning, the strange labyrinth of bureaucracy, the mess of red tape, underfunded agencies and corruption make doing business lawfully a complicated and discouraging task that, in the end, prevents business owners from entering global markets. The process can take months, even if one consults with legal and financial advisers and follows all the correct procedures. Obtaining the

required permits and licenses and thoroughly ver-
ifying the registration and notification of operations'
commencement is a nightmare. That's why numerous
investors with the resources to elevate our country to
newer heights have chosen to shelve their entrepreneurial skills or apply them in neighboring countries.

I understand these problems from personal experience; I have explored many ways to start a business in Haiti myself. When I considered the lengths
to which some must go to protect their space in the
market, their small kingdom, and the current government's inability to tackle corrupt and criminal practices, I opted, instead, to preserve my integrity and
sanity. Upon her graduation from business school in
the United States, unlike many who have left Haiti
permanently, my friend Christine returned home and
took a job with a prominent company. After settling
into her new position as a director, she discovered
that the company was not making any effort to rein-
vest profits, leaving the cash on hand. She remembers
the odor of cardboard and currency baking in midday
sunlight from the cash room, as if the company was
making an indictment of the present banking system.

Christine had the authority to invest on behalf
of her employer. She got all the necessary licenses
and registered a subsidiary enterprise. The lesson she learned was that there was no "right" way

to do things in Haiti. Even when paying the fees to obtain all required licenses and all the taxes—contributing one's fair share—one still has no recourse when others take criminal actions to eliminate you as competition. She invested the piles of cash that her employer had on hand to create a microlending program to encourage self-sufficiency and eradicate poverty through female entrepreneurship. Her model was structured to import a popular laundry soap and set up distribution through a network of women all over the country. Each woman received cases of soap at a wholesale price equivalent to five hundred dollars as a business loan. The profit margin was 30 percent, of which they repaid 10 percent with the loan principal.

The program became immensely popular, and the soaps sold out quickly. It only made sense for Christine to expand. At the time, 150 women were involved in the program. Her goal was to double the number of participants. The cases of soap ordered reflected the number of women the program hoped to serve.

But another company dominated Haiti's soap market at that time. The owner was afraid that the microlending program was becoming serious competition. He bribed a customs agent to hold back the soap for the program just long enough to inject them with ink. When the soap reached consumers, they got ink on their clothes. This stunt ruined the reputation of a brand that was once so popular, discrediting the microlending program. Her investment lost, the authorities unwilling to step in to help, Christine felt powerless. The police, including the justice system that prosecutes criminal acts, is underfunded, corrupt and unable to act.

What happened to Christine is not an isolated incident to illustrate my remark regarding the creation of wealth in Haiti; it is the story of every Haitian small business owner. Their opportunities for success are either criminal or unethical, in an economy that has been immoral since its inception, not meant to include everyone. Here, a program for empowerment, economic development and women's issues that should have grown into a well-functioning system that serves the country's greater good was caught in a scurry for wealth that promoted the status quo.

✦ ✦ ✦

One day, as I drove past the most prominent market near my residence in Pétion-Ville, I stopped short to witness the degradation of the twelve mangoes a woman had on display for sale. She sat on a *marmiton*, fist clenched under her chin to support her tired head, waiting for a customer who would be kind enough to buy her not-so-fresh produce. My heart heavy, I engaged in a light conversation with her as she packed some fruit for me. I learned that Marlene was the head of her household, a family of five.

Our rural poverty hides in open space, right under our noses; 60 percent of female-led households live below the poverty line and are overrepresented in the informal and vulnerable employment market, just like Marlene. The loosely formed, open-air markets in Pétion-Ville are swimming with them, functioning freely and collectively as a symbol of civil defiance against any structured arrangement or government interference. The burble of their voices mudded like the slow and discreet music of an isolated waterfall. The sights, the smells, the noise, the tents, the colors might overwhelm you. Women like Marlene come from near and far to sell all sorts of goods. They brave the wee hours of the morning and the insecurities lurking behind tall walls at night. They are mothers, sisters, daughters, sometimes children.

For Marlene and her family, life has always been a struggle that has taken many forms. She told me she used to work as a maid. She had to quit after her boss insisted that she perform sexual favors in exchange for a raise. Silenced and burdened by the duality of economic and social oppression, she resorted to self-employment as a street vendor, earning less but preserving her dignity.

Preserving one's dignity comes at a high price many women bear daily to provide for themselves and their children's sustenance. Without access to reasonable health care, quality public education, affordable housing and good public transportation, life remains particularly troublesome for disenfranchised and impoverished women like Marlene. They worry about raising their children to be productive members of society.

Thus, we cannot expect to grow as a country without mentioning women's empowerment. Women in Haiti have faced inequalities for far too long. The treatment they have been subjected to has not only hurt them but also their families, their communities and the country as a whole. One thing is abundantly clear: We will not increase our economic output without working harder to achieve gender equality.

Similarly, since the beginning of time, human beings have tried to place themselves above others. Our discrimination against women is usually based on the assumption that they are inferior to men and can only fulfill specific societal roles that are also undervalued. I am in bitter opposition to this patriarchal notion deeply rooted in our culture and fueled by discriminatory practices against women both in the family and in the public sphere. They experience many constraints to achieving political participation and high leadership positions—intimidation, harassment and sexual violence—and they are less likely to have access to social and judicial protections.

Marlene recounted the physical abuse she endured from her former husband. One day things got so violent, her screams caused neighbors to fill the sidewalk outside their homes. An older woman asked a police officer to intervene as he stood idly by among the bystanders, watching the scene unfold. The officer contemptuously responded, "You want me to do what exactly? Am I the one who feeds her every day?"

This despicable response is why female victims of discrimination, harassment and violence in Haiti are not inclined to seek legal protection. Widespread indifference to these problems in our culture represent a significant obstacle to women gaining access to justice. Victims and their families are often mistreated in their quest to right the injustices done to them, their social and economic standing usually cited as the reason why they are not entitled to justice.

Many of our nation's women are marginalized, their perspectives and experiences commonly overlooked. Their positions seldom reflect their aptitude or level of education. We must learn to make room for female expertise. While Haiti's societal structure places men in a providing role, women are usually the decision-makers about children's education, finances and other family areas. Struggling merely to survive, they often have no time or energy to think about public policy. And their voices do not carry far in the public debate. The government ought to play an essential role in establishing the parameters necessary to empower women, a critical element in the fight against poverty and sustainable development. As such, the increased political representation of women in politics, business, education, health care and business is central to a prosperous Haiti.

Haitian feminists have entered the fight because women are more likely than their male colleagues to be victims of exploitation, abuse and sexual and other forms of violence. They seek to raise women's employment throughout the government from 30 to 50 percent, assuming that economic growth inevitably leads to social development and gender equality.

But economic growth alone will not suffice. If that were true, the economic growth of the United States would have left that country better off in terms of gender equality over the past seventy-five years. That country too still deals with many of the same issues Haiti does. Therefore, the ultimate path to empowering women is through the political process, which is to change gender relations and shift the hierarchical relationships of society.

In retrospect, my family was no stranger to

Marlene's struggles. Dad, having migrated to the United States, left Mom behind as acting head of our household. Though she was never a victim of spousal abuse, the worsening conditions brought on by the 1991 commercial embargo severely impacted us. The remittances from Dad allowed my siblings and me to attend some of the best schools when others were not so well positioned. But the soaring costs of public transportation forced us to ride our bicycles as a substitute. We lived in Valère, where our parents could afford to build a home, fifteen kilometers away from the good schools in Les Cayes. We often experienced trying moments journeying back and forth on a dirt road to reach the private school we attended, Frère Odile Joseph. At times our skins felt corroded by the friction of our haunches against the rubber seats of those bicycles. Rainy days were the worst.

Nevertheless, we were able to reach school on time with brazen aplomb. It is not as if we had much choice. The headmaster would find creative ways to chastise students who could not get to school on time, ignoring their socioeconomic inconveniences. My teachers rarely forgave us if we showed up with unfinished homework or unmemorized lessons because we could not study in the dark. They would have us write hundreds of repetitive lines as punishment. They penalized us for the poverty we inherited.

How could we be blamed for the lack of transportation and electricity in our country?

I grew resentful of that life. Some of my schoolmates would kick rocks to curb the depression caused by the school's methods of discipline. Every coping mechanism I later employed to deal with oppression, I learned from deflecting the behavior of my supposedly nurturing teachers. Optimism is often what sets apart children and families who undergo hardships. Life imbues them with an abundance of hope that things can change. My best friend, Jacobsen, who today is a medical doctor, and I wrote poetry to escape memories of these ordeals, expressing our hopes and dreams. We were young, though we had much to learn in life; we were eager to rush into the future to meet better days. We evolved beyond our struggles into two active contributors to our country's progress. Looking back at the oppression, resentment and despair we endured growing up—a repetition of which has ruined many good children—we deem ourselves lucky to have been able to escape the unfortunate path to becoming like the men who caused Haiti so much pain. We owe much of our successes today to the teachers, who, among the pillars of our communities, continued to teach in precarious conditions to support us, the seniors in our neighborhood who had authority over the youth, keeping us in line beyond the nucleus of our family structure.

In those days, the school a child attended directly correlated with the financial means of their parents or where they lived. Although the Constitution guarantees the right to an education, the implementation of education was mostly private. Considering that more than 80 percent of Haiti's schools are still private today, nothing has changed. This represents a severe issue we continue to face with our education system. The concept of a stellar education in Haiti becomes laughable compared to international standards. Haiti's long struggles share two common denominators: lack of education and increased poverty.

The inverse was supposed to be the answer to our problems, the solution to Marlene's plight. I used to listen to the debates about strengthening the middle class, as if Haiti ever had one. The middle class is an economic engine that does not emerge overnight or through cheap political sound bites. It is created over time through deliberate policy measures and investments that will reflect an educated population. When we think of the middle class, we need to think of a social and economic cornerstone, a symbol of our way of life—having financial security, raising a family with a reasonable standard of living, building a stable future for the next generation.

When I returned from the diaspora, I expected us to have stopped treating education as part of our industrial economy and make it the public service it should be. We say we want a future for our children, but we leave the education system in the hands of the free market and tell parents it's important to send their kids to school. Along with the expense of tuition, many families cannot afford the uniforms and supplies needed for their kids to go to school. The delusional way we treat education flabbergasts me. I wanted the government to set and enforce a permanent policy to empower women and their children, to ensure that schools are of the same standard and accessibility regardless of location.

President Michel Martelly campaigned on that promise but failed to deliver. As he undoubtedly managed to rid himself of that disappointment, the biggest mistake we make as a nation is expecting education reform from leaders whom the same system has failed. With most of our schools being nonpublic, and public education being of low quality, our current leaders have had their share of struggles through their own educational experiences. The curriculum for both elementary and higher education did not prepare them for our country's challenges. As a result of poor education and lack of access to information, they fail to comprehend how society's interests affect their own. We have not created a nation of critical thinkers.

Over the years, Marlene became one of the thousands who looked for economic opportunity elsewhere. She scraped together money from friends and family and left for Chile, a country that opened its arms to our people without visas. Like the Dominican Republic, Brazil and other countries, Chile strategically designed and implemented attractive immigration policies befitting their economic growth needs through the exploitation of cheap labor, only to isolate and marginalize those Haitian immigrants.

✦ ✦ ✦

The migration of the diaspora to opportunity-rich countries has depleted essential human capital and affected our prospects for economic development. The brain drain that began in the late 1960s has eroded our labor force, and 70 percent of our skilled workers still live abroad. The country has lost more than 100,000 workers in the past five years alone, and many say they are considering leaving. The loss of so many skilled workers has had a ripple effect. Every year there are fewer people to deliver vital public services, drive economic growth and articulate calls for greater democracy and human development. Our political leaders' intuitive response is to reduce the scale of emigration to ease the brain and capacity drain issue. However, one-size-fits-all measures aimed at limiting mobility is not the most efficient way to tackle the problem.

Instead, better methodologies are needed to identify where the brain drain undermines Haiti's ability to meet the millennium development goals. We need to develop a strategy to keep our skilled and educated workers by making our country an attractive place for those in the diaspora to return to. Yet a meaningful solution lies in tapping the vital resource the diaspora represents. The shortage of teachers, doctors, scientists and engineers has slowed the country's development and ripped a massive hole in the economy. Why must we put so many obstacles in the way of a group that shares the same desire for a prosperous Haiti as those who live here full-time?

In the collective mind of the diaspora is the idea that their flight is temporary. Someday there will be a return ticket; they will wake up one morning to read the news that there is a stable and competent government in Haiti and come flying home to aid in the reconstruction of the homeland. I was one of those poised to serve the motherland but not enticed to leave a full-time career in the United States for short-term conditions and limited prospects for growth.

Many of my friends from the diaspora returned before me, to take underpaid positions in Haiti. Their short time in-country was often frivolously wasted; they accomplished extraordinarily little to push Haiti forward. What a terrible shame. When other members of the diaspora think about all the things they can achieve, they don't care about the personal hardship they might have to endure as long as they have a clear path by which to contribute meaningfully to Haiti's revival. A set of rules and metrics is all they demand.

Haiti can only depend on so many diaspora members returning out of pure patriotism—the kind of patriotism that led me to abandon everything in the United States to move back and work on a political campaign without remuneration for over a year. I still remember those nights my friend Stephane Vincent and I worked on digital strategies for the government and policies for e-Governance when he lived in New York, even before we met in person. Our desire to contribute to the efforts to rebuild Haiti united us. We both moved back without much preparation or orientation, a massive step into the unknown. I experienced many personal losses being back in Haiti—family and friends. Everyone called me crazy. But the homeland taught me to suffer without weakening. Our greatest pains are always silent anyway; I do not know what killed it, the distance or the silence.

Despite it all, my commitment to Haiti will never waiver.

In the homeland, the local culture has a way of ostracizing members of the diaspora. At first, in my interactions with friends, my pronunciation would be made fun of, little reminders pointed to that conjured up the feeling that I did not belong. The subtext of their jibes seemed to suggest that my time away might have stripped me of my essence as a Haitian. Similarly, fulfilling basic needs that seemed reasonable while living abroad, such as having a home with hot water and air conditioning, would leave me feeling disillusioned by the country's realities. I almost became a foreigner in my homeland.

I met Naikema, who would become like family during that struggle. She had been back in Haiti for some time and had experienced the bicultural pull with an incredible capacity for maintaining a comfortable bond between Montreal and Port-au-Prince. She and I would argue about everything but always upheld our shared passion for Haiti. We would sit on the rocking chairs on her home's balcony having endless debates about the Haiti of our dreams. She too believes that we are part of the new generation who can change things. That now was the time when there was no more important task for our country than for its full-time residents and the diaspora to work in unison to remedy our problems and set our country on course to exceptional heights.

My optimism has often been a point of divergence between my friends and me. Djenane would call me a visionary, crazy for Haiti. That was her way of making me feel out of touch with the local experience. She feared the biggest obstacle to changing Haiti is its past—or rather, our perception of its history. Nonetheless, she would admit that I always had a passionate and valid argument.

That type of idealistic divergence and social segregation was no different from what I encountered living in America. There were two things about which I could never say no to my parents: school and church. That is mostly the effect our culture has on us. Trying to study and absorb the English language in an often violent and under-resourced public school that lacked understanding of my culture was no easy feat. As a result, many of my compatriots struggled with academic achievement. Our Black American classmates did not make it easier for us. They often joked about the vast numbers of "boat people" arriving on Florida's shores. They refused to consider us their equals, in part because of our foreign accent, and the adverse publicity that had tarnished Haitians' image all over the world—the widespread labeling of us all as a group at risk for AIDS. In suburban Dartmouth, my white friends identified me as a Black man. In Dorchester, my Haitian friends, who functioned and interacted mostly within their culture, accused me of being acculturated. In their view, I was the "other."

The race relations and the culture shock I experienced in America made for a difficult integration. In my attempt to balance multiple cultures, I found myself transitioning out of some proud Caribbean practices, such as greeting everyone individually when entering a room. I surrendered to American teens' peer pressure, living with reckless abandon, attending wild parties, wearing expensive clothing and striving for personal fulfillment through material wealth. A sense of inner despair often accompanied those quests for pleasure.

Thinking of the way my family fought to redefine success in an America determined to deprive us of it, I recognize that Dad probably had it worse. From the long stretch of beltway connecting our neighborhood with the highway system, he would drive sixty miles to work in the city. He called it "investing against the odds," an impressive work ethic he transferred to my brother and me before he passed away. He was the first in his family to graduate college, earning a degree that should have made him successful. As he worked hard to live up to America's depiction of the "perfect" family, he developed a strong distaste for life abroad.

His attempts to assimilate, to break economic barriers, caused his alienation when the realities proved too restrictive.

However, Dad refused to accept these drawbacks as his children's inheritance. He was always ready to tackle life ambitiously, setting high goals for himself and his family. He forced us to study and work harder, dare to want more and always give back. He emphasized our ethnic background to the full extent to make sure we would never be disconnected from our cultural identity. He counted the days until we could go back to Haiti, focusing all his savings, investments and retirement plans there. The moment we graduated from college, Dad did return to the homeland, only to regress to dire circumstances that would cost him his life just a year later in a motorcycle accident. I still struggle to cope with the emotional aftermath of his death. I was the firstborn, and the load of his financial obligations fell on my shoulders; he was the one who kept his other relatives afloat. I would weep uncontrollably on my mother's shoulder each time his absence haunted us.

As members of the diaspora struggle to dispel paralyzing myths and rebuild life abroad, the country they have left behind continues to be a source of suffering. Our diaspora is as unwelcome at home as they are overseas. Their lives consist of constant disruption. They continue to enter host countries as unwanted immigrants, Black minorities, an ethno-linguistic group that is usually isolated. Meanwhile, in the motherland, the Constitution reinforces their legal, economic and sociopolitical segregation.

This does not allow the country to move forward with the assistance of its diaspora. Government officials love the status quo. Both the ministry of foreign affairs and the ministry for Haitians living abroad are unwilling to create a strong network to unite all diaspora members to channel their voices directly to the Haitian cause. The expanding diaspora group remains eager to share political influence but cannot exercise the right to vote in elections.

I do not understand how this system survived for so long while impeding the human desire for inclusion. But no matter how secluded life in either Boston or Port-au-Prince wants me to be, I will always be Haitian. I was born of parents who endured the dangers of coup d'états, the privations of dictatorships and embargoes brought on by democracy, who saw radical visionaries who promised better days but brought only extensive destruction. I am the son of great-grandparents who proudly exhibited devotion to duty and service to our military, pioneers, voodoo priests and community leaders in Dolin, where the voices of their distant sanctuary drums, the piercing sound of bamboos and horns, would proclaim to neighbors that the dances would soon begin on hot August nights.

I grew up with both Haitian and American values and moral standards, which, in my opinion, are the hallmarks of human decency and excellence. In Haiti, I learned superstitions that will remain eternally part of me. In America, I learned to control my destiny and not leave the future to chance; to allow my dreams to be bigger than my fears, my actions louder than my words and my faith stronger than my feelings. At my birth, my grandmother had me wear unique beads to ward off evil spirits. Later, I embraced the leading edges of science and logic. I still respect and obey my elders, walking a fine line because I believe that my wrongdoings have the power to affect the reputation of my family name. Still, I was raised the American way, as a free thinker who can look you in the eye and tell it like it is.

While the existing system continues to impede our integration, the diaspora plays an extraordinary role in Haiti's economic infrastructure. Dollars flow from the diaspora as remittances that exceed the country's exports, estimated to account for a quarter of its gross domestic product. Yet the same financial system through which the diaspora sends money leaves them longing for inclusion. The diaspora has no access to credit in Haiti, a discouraging roadblock for doing business there. Without adequate financing, members of the diaspora are not able to build companies that will last decades. Consequently, their business initiatives tend to be micro or small in scale, and many of them function as informal operations, relying mostly on personal relationships.

Another area that requires contortion is that remittances from the diaspora are not funding sustainable sectors of our economy. There is no denying that the money transfers from the diaspora make a significant contribution to the homeland; there is ample evidence suggesting that remittances improve household functions, which means more spending on the part of consumers. Yet the impact of financial remittances on poverty is complex and nuanced. The positive impact remains primarily on an individual basis. At a macro level, they

The diaspora should not be content with constitutional reform as a pathway to sociopolitical and economic integration

promote problematic issues on national consumption patterns and adverse effects on the gourde. Because the country lacks economic and migrant capital management policies, enabling environments to enhance the development impact of money transfers, the diaspora remains economically excluded from the homeland's sustainable development. We have focused expansion plans on short-term industrial and assembly work from companies wary of establishing a permanent presence, but the low-wage jobs they bring are always temporary.

A pressing priority for the future must be to create a more structured, intelligently financed way to mobilize and engage the talented diaspora in rebuilding a better country. We should design collective remittance programs to address our shortcomings in economic and social infrastructure, involving health, education, recreation and other public services. The diaspora certainly has the financial capacity to help facilitate better development and enhance human capital.

Therefore, the diaspora should not be content with constitutional reform as a pathway to sociopolitical and economic integration. The government needs a national plan that outlines the roles and functions the diaspora can play in executing development strategies. The diaspora is home to more than one million people with advanced engineering and computer science degrees, just the skills needed to rebuild Haiti. Thanks to their international connections and a wealth of expertise, our ex-pats can bridge the gap between local and international assistance by strengthening local capacities and increasing the appropriate use of aid.

✦ ✦ ✦

Many nongovernmental and foreign aid organizations have behaved, while in our country, more as businesses. There exists little in the way of oversight. When the earthquake happened, and the floods came, and the hurricanes followed, donation requests bombarded the international community. Planes and boats loaded with aid workers and volunteers poured from the harbors and airports throughout the country. Everyone seemed eager to help.

The truth is, too many aid organizations have looted Haiti. They depleted the government of qualified personnel by offering higher wages, benefits and better working conditions. The foreign professionals channeled through those organizations took advantage of local corruption to improve their own lifestyles, robbed the government of its legitimacy and distorted the local economy by driving up the cost of living. Now, years after the earthquake, no organization has been able to present a detailed performance report demonstrating the added value of their interventions.

Since 2006, Haiti has received more than sixteen

billion dollars in development assistance, making it the third-largest aid recipient in the Americas. Over the years, the country has become aid-dependent, receiving relatively large amounts of foreign money representing close to 13 percent of the gross domestic product. Haiti remains one of the most underdeveloped countries, with the lowest human development indicators. It is safe to conclude that foreign aid has not accelerated development. Compared to the lack of improvement of socioeconomic indicators, the gauge of foreign aid allocated to Haiti raises severe questions of aid effectiveness.

At the International Donors Conference held on March 31, 2010, more than five billion dollars was pledged for Haiti's recovery. In partnership with the Haitian government, officials of international organizations, multilateral lenders and major donors created the Interim Haitian Reconstruction Commission to adhere to "the principles of aid effectiveness." Nevertheless, as cash poured in, the partnership failed. Aid organizations followed their own agendas, excluding the government and civil society. So, what was the vision of aid organizations for Haiti? They prevented the sustainable development of Haiti for the sake of continuing to aid. None of the nongovernmental and foreign aid organizations that have operated in Haiti have left behind a power plant, a highway or anything sustainable. As Jonathan M. Katz says in his book *The Big Truck That Went By: How the World Came to Save Haiti and Left a Disaster Behind*, "Two centuries of turmoil and foreign meddling had left a Haitian state so anemic it could not even count how many citizens it had... There was no way for Haitians to appeal an NGO decision, prosecute a bad soldier, or vote an unwanted USAID project out of a neighborhood."[*]

When President Moïse assumed office, he took a strong stance against Haiti's so-called partners to reduce our foreign dependence. In his view, this aid had become institutions for underdevelopment and acerbic critics of the government when their interests were threatened, perpetuating the nation's continued exploitation. It was evident that a courageous leadership should repudiate the practice of spending millions of aid dollars every year without substantive progress to show for it. The government's task is to ensure that any aid provided facilitates self-reliance; it must always include elements that empower the Haitian people. We will not achieve the dream of becoming a first-world nation standing atop piles of donated Red Cross boxes, but by producing for ourselves.

While assessments of aid performances have been unsatisfactory for decades, indicating that Haiti has been failed again and again, it would be criminal to blame these nongovernmental and foreign aid organizations alone. The Haitian government is equally responsible for the disappointments. Poor governance, political instability and weak public institutional capacity for coordination over the past several decades have created an environment that is not favorable to aid effectiveness.

It is not only that foreign aid is not effective in Haiti; it is reliant on it. Foreign aid is a highly profitable transaction between those who come rushing to our rescue and the government officials who welcome them after each tragedy. It is the profit of poverty, where the two leverage our debt and disaster to push through a series of ruinous policies. For Haiti to receive aid, organizations force our lawmakers to privatize public assets, reduce tariffs on imports and deregulate businesses. These strategies paved the way for our political and economic dependence on imports, aid and a few prominent families to monopolize the nation's economy—and thus its politics. It is the profit of poverty, where our dependence benefits them more than our autonomy would.

✦ ✦ ✦

Haiti can regain its vibrancy and soul as a country; its economy can boom and become more competitive, and we can curb our issues with corruption. It can modernize to reinforce public institutions to support our foreign policy initiatives and deliver the services that our people deserve in the most efficient manner possible. The Chinese believe that crisis and opportunity are tied together, two sides of the same coin. The constant turmoil in Haiti is an opportunity to reexamine how we move forward smarter, better prepared and stronger together. When I tweeted that jobs must accompany any substantial increase in the price of essential goods, it was the instigation that led to my political consciousness. I realized that no native Haitian or outsider could pinpoint any sector of the economy, standing alone, that has a substantial positive impact on Haiti. All industries must integrate and build sustainably together.

Mom and Dad used to talk about their parents' struggles growing up. They thought whatever my generation has gone through pales in comparison to the hardships previous generations endured. It was hard to argue against those testimonials. The evidence of our misfortunes seemed vast and stretched over a long period. But I believe that past generations often dismiss our current conditions for fear that the right answer might be an acknowledgment that they had failed by not leaving behind a better Haiti for us.

It is said that history repeats itself; we are doomed

to replicate cycles of misfortune. However persuasive the idiom might sound, today, more than anything, we want to be better than our immediate past. We dream of a Haiti where it is incumbent on all of us to do everything possible to ensure everyone's well-being. We are a people rich in culture and accomplishment. Our young see the potential and want nothing more than to see our country reach and exceed her dreams. They simply want to live in a country where we can all succeed if we try. It is the legacy we must leave for Haiti's future generations.

I have had the chance to travel to different parts of Africa, the Middle East, North and South America. In the glamorous brew of hidden details about their advancements, governments play a fundamental role in empowering their citizens. Governments are rarely in total control of the processes of empowerment. There is a chorus of other actors, some degree of external influence from foreign investors, aid donors and international institutions with a significant impact on decision-making. In the state of Massachusetts, I served on the development boards of many local associations. I was also committed to the missions of several charitable organizations in the city of New Bedford, working to empower communities. I have met many social influencers, community organizers, faith leaders and intellectuals who worked to promote the framework and policies for people to empower themselves, to encourage interactions with business associations and trade unions.

Nongovernmental organizations can be our real partners in development. For the perception to change what is possible, even expected, for Haiti, we must implement a national strategic aid framework to align donor and government priorities. The solutions to our problems should come from the people themselves. We must take control of our own destiny. There can be no more waiting for saviors to swoop in with magic wands, dictating their terms. We can create an aid coordination structure to ensure better management by adopting a donor strategy focused on improving governance, delivering social services and strengthening state capacity. The government must have the power to enforce laws in a meaningful way, from policing to prosecution.

More of the same is not the answer. Making changes around the edges, bringing more projects onboard— giving the government no greater reach, impact and surety for its authority—will do nothing to alter our current trajectory on a course for more of the same. More of the same will only bring an ongoing progression of collective misery. Only a few will raise themselves from poverty to more prominent, more powerful, wealthier lives. Our main reforms must have the goal of discouraging the practice of becoming wealthy through illegal and immoral ways alone. Simple changes to laws, words on a page, are not enough. Our government must secure an honorable course to prosperity by ensuring the rule of law. If anything, our government's greatest sin has been the systematic lack of implementation of numerous plans and the weak enforcement of a long list of regulations.

Ascending from this kind of poverty is all about creating well-paying jobs and other economic activity that stimulates growth that, most importantly, is safeguarded by a strong government able to prevent corrupt practices. We can make real progress if we create possibilities for people who are not currently participating in the economy. Our people's ingenuity and entrepreneurial spirit are incredible and are missed by investors because the global narrative does not position Haiti as a haven for start-ups. Our laws must reflect the reality that being open for business means that businesses are rapidly opening, that the impediments are low. Assistance from the Haitian government and outside organizations working in a coordinated way to sustain business development will build a twenty-first-century economy.

We must define the prospect for our economic growth by the prodigious development of production poles, the profitability of our trade balance and the volume of money in circulation and investment. Haiti should in no way be dependent, dominated or vulnerable to the point of being unable to decide for itself. To achieve a competitive economy and to transform the country into a new, empowered, emerging force, a leader in innovation, environmental sustainability and socioeconomic justice, Haiti needs to make strategic investments in:

Infrastructure/Environment

• A public transportation overhaul: build a highway network and a public transportation system to interconnect the country's ten geographical departments, leading to better access to our ports, airports, historical sites, caves, seaside resorts and waterfalls to enhance all areas of economic attractions.

• Major reform of the energy sector prioritizing renewable energy through public-private partnerships to ensure substantial cost reduction in infrastructure investment, improve economic growth and strengthen competitiveness.

• A cutting-edge communication network for better Internet connectivity, information sharing and communication technology services.

• A health system that finances, organizes and delivers the best care in light of our lack of available resources and competing needs.

• Development/improvement of water, sewer and stormwater systems to enable our cities and metropolitan areas to function as centers of commerce, industry, entertainment and human habitation.

• Government programs to restore a green infrastructure: Rebuilding the country's depleted natural resources by planting millions of trees to prevent flood and soil erosion. A fully integrated waste management and recycling infrastructure to collect waste, clean up plastic pollution and manage landfills responsibly.

Education/Social Reform

• A world-class public education system—advanced, progressive and responsive to the needs of the country and the global economy—with equal access to student loan and grant programs facilitating upward mobility and job-skills training to increase the ability of marginalized groups to move up the career ladder and level the playing field.

• Comprehensive safety-net programs, quality public

housing, affordable health insurance and retirement plans to protect families from the impact of economic distresses, natural disasters and other crises, and to lift millions of Haitians out of deep poverty.

Economic Reform

• Take control of revenue through the modernization of Customs and the Authorité Portuaire Nationale (APN), modernization of the Direction Générale des Impots (DGI), the total reform of the national lottery system, the creation of a national circulation center and reforming the Office d'Assurance Vehicules Contre Tiers (OAVCT).

• Redesign banking infrastructure to provide all citizens and businesses with access to a fully functional, national credit system as we ensure reasonable macroeconomic stability through monetary policies that effectively manage inflation and interest rates.

• Mobilize part of our gross domestic product in productive private investments to allow Haiti to gain access to attractive markets on favorable terms, to insert itself into global value chains while engaging in responsive public-private dialogues.

• Unlock entrepreneurial potential for growth by promoting innovation and entrepreneurship through favorable tax programs. Encourage the emergence of businesses of all kinds to create jobs, reduce unemployment and gradually improve the living conditions of the population.

• Initiate a supermarket management system under municipal governments' supervision to promote upward socioeconomic mobility as we regulate all trading activities to unify the informal economy with the formal structure.

Sustainable Tourism

• Institute competitive tourism infrastructure and suprastructure projects as determinants of development, government partnerships and well-defined public policy to diversify the tourism industry to promote thriving arts, cultural and entertainment (cinema, sports, music) scenes reflective of the unique character, culture and historical heritage and resources of Haiti.

Rule of Law

• Allow for constitutional reform to strengthen the justice system and democracy, promoting the rule of law to ensure a well-supervised and rich ecosystem of financial institutions and instruments.

• Restructure and empower a web of law enforcement institutions to fight corruption, promote public safety and uphold the rule of law for a society of peace, security and prosperity.

✦ ✦ ✦

Our people live two lives—one in which they seek out their hopes and another in which the deterioration of their standard of living pushes them to suspend their morals to survive. High unemployment, rising inflation that erodes earnings for those who are employed and substantial disparities in poverty plague the country. Its strains are even suburbanized, so deeply rooted in our society they crawled through the gates of the National Palace, concentrating themselves only a few feet away from the president's office and his excellency's lawful exuberance, as income inequality, lack of access to adequate health insurance and housing issues fully displayed the vulnerability of employees as the poorest members of our nation. By my first year working for the administration, I had already found the predatory and immoral practices to which the state subjugates its employees appalling. Some people are being paid as little as fifteen thousand gourdes a month. In a segment in my journal, I referenced the landscape as "the silence of misery." As my friend, Gaimcy, once put it, "The pay sucks, you get no respect and the checks are always late."

The executive level of government is meant to be the pinnacle of society, a respected, prestigious and exclusive working environment even in a developing country. But it was where I learned about the defenselessness of some of my brothers and sisters: drivers, mail couriers, maids, gardeners, administrative aides, advisers who couldn't afford to feed their families. It was where I met Yves-Marie Bance, who worked as a logistical aid in the Palace. He suffered from a medical condition that required continuous treatment. Bance asked for an advance on his pay to procure his medication while he waited for his late paycheck. Though he emphasized the seriousness of his predicament and the likelihood of it resulting in his death, his claim was denied. He passed away two days later. He never had the chance to collect that last paycheck.

Many senior cabinet members, including the

president, live with a cognitive blindness to the difficulties associated with low-wage work or institutionalized discrimination based on social classes. Their perception remains that people in poverty are indolent, careless, haven't made the right decisions. This results in the government's weak institutional capacity and bad leadership in their ability to design inclusive and compulsory national social programs to help struggling families. The reality is that finding opportunity without help from families, friends, community and government is virtually impossible.

Bance's tragedy was not a question of low wages; it was about living conditions. It was not a question of inadequate health insurance, but a question of hope for the future; a loud echo of Marlene's story of destitution and many other families like hers that have no safety net. I once asked a senior cabinet member one question pertaining to the incident: "How can we be deemed worthy of leading the nation when its sons and daughters closest to us are suffering in numbers?" She never found an answer to a rhetorical question only intended to shock the conscience.

Growing up, I emerged from a dense culture of interdependence based on articulated, shared, more-than-economic values and nonexistent government safety nets. Social programs such as food subsidies would have alleviated our burden of poverty. I often survived on small weekly credit from Rosette's corner store; I am quite sure her lemonade and warm loaves of bread kept me alive when I would otherwise have collapsed. Many years after I returned from the diaspora, her dream of starting a modern bakery still had not manifested; a failure to access business credit tipped the scales for her, as it did for many others who hoped to open small businesses across the nation, the playing field remaining far from level.

What the leading nations have attained for themselves, we have not been able to secure: the right to live in dignity and participate actively in the building of a more equal society, the right to social benefits that have proliferated over centuries, the right not to suffer fallout from the bad faith of the institutions overseeing retirement funds belonging to every citizen. As Adam Smith said in *The Wealth of Nations*, "No society can surely be flourishing and happy, of which the far greater part of the members are poor and miserable."*

Haiti needs comprehensive safety net programs, quality public housing, affordable health insurance and retirement plans to protect individuals and families from the impact of economic distresses, natural disasters and other crises to lift millions of Haitians out of deep poverty. The aim is to replace the weak social projects tied to the promotion of political parties and elected officials—projects that often vanish at the end of an administration's term—with permanent programs that are guaranteed to exist outside political dissonance, programs that solve the real problems of both children and students, seniors and women and the disenfranchised. Our social programs must be divorced from politics as usual and maintained as constitutional guarantees carried out irrespective of whatever administration assumes power. These programs must be national and operated through uncorrupt agencies disconnected from the political structure, a part of the governmental apparatus itself.

Haiti's existing safety net programs are as ineffective as they are corrupt, serving as cash cows for elected officials. The complacency of the directors of those institutions is often detrimental to the very efficiency of the latter. The Office Nationale d'Assurance-Vieillesse (ONA)'s banking structure is a recent example as repeated scandals sully the reputation of the institution. It was nearly dismantled by influential Parliament members granting exorbitant loans to friends, paramours and family members for terms that exceeded the borrower's life expectancy. Yet taxpayers who contribute to ONA hardly benefit from its services. Furthermore, most projects funded by the institution have proven unsustainable and ineffective.

Existing housing programs have proven to be

wasteful when they attempt to solve the issues they were meant to address. Houses built to support struggling families remained unassigned for so long they were eventually abandoned. We have a pressing need to build affordable housing across the country, through a national strategy to introduce zoning and laws on subsidies. Before we can have an empowered and industrious populace, they must be fed and housed. Existing poverty reduction programs around the world provide models of how to combine transit, housing and other key components. The survival tactics of poverty must be unlearned through subsidized housing and food supplement programs with the benchmark for graduation out of the program being self-sufficiency.

Our housing issue can be transformed in tandem with employment efforts if we cultivate relationships with small developers, giving preference to those interested in community building. These small-scale developers can be instrumental in building on walkable infrastructure while employing local workers and keeping their profits in the community. Again, existing poverty-reduction programs around the world provide models based on the transit, housing and employment trifecta. Households in poverty spend more on basic needs: transportation, food, telecommunications and water. Those expenses can be reduced through proven programs that yield sustainable results.

✦ ✦ ✦

Improving our public health system is of significant importance to the socioeconomic development of the country. The 1987 Constitution recognizes a fundamental right to health and the State's obligation to guarantee it for all. But the deterioration in our socioeconomic makeup and the underfunding of health-care infrastructure and medical equipment have created a disturbing albeit surmountable challenge. The sector that comprises public institutions and private insurance agencies and providers lags behind international standards and continues to fail the most vulnerable in our society. As the Ministère de la Santé Publique et de la Population (MSPP) provides health services to the nonsalaried population and the Office d'Assurance Accidents du Travail, Maladie et Maternité (OFATMA) addresses the employed, children and the elderly who face financial barriers to accessing health-care services, remain exposed to more risks.

The main challenge faced by our health system remains the provision for comprehensive health services with financial protection to all the population.

Haiti needs a health system to finance, organize and ensure equal access to the best care. In light of our lack of available resources and competing priorities, making such a health system a reality requires that the government maintain significant improvements in our medical insurance legal infrastructure, review policy on the pharmaceutical industry, use new health financing modalities, undertake hospital reforms and introduce innovative health legislation guiding a robust health network and information system that looks to cutting-edge technologies to deliver the best and most affordable universal coverage and health-care science has to offer.

The government's subsidized voluntary insurance program through OFATMA warrants new, comprehensive legislation mandating its health and social protection for all, with premiums based on a sliding scale. By gradually ensuring coverage for all and facilitating access to care, the health system will ultimately fulfill its constitutional obligation. This goal will not be met without additional financial resources—mostly public—and an effort to restructure and strengthen existing state hospitals, health centers, clinics and other medical facilities, including in rural areas, as we build new, modern hospitals with appropriate ambulance services.

We must also strengthen the Ministry of Health at

all levels to regulate all matters related to the pharmaceutical industry, from overseeing drug registrations, applying control on imports and administering inspections of private drug manufacturers and pharmacies. Only then can our many talented physicians, nurses and medical staffers, at home and around the diaspora, transform our country into a center of affordable health tourism with state-of-the-art information infrastructure that expands beyond the concept of treatment to preventative measures.

These are the steps to forming an arrangement of competent medical teams, specialized human resources and managerial capacity to guarantee and improve the health of the Haitian population. Aside from its organizational structure, our reforms must account for better coordination of health aides by articulating intelligent, transparent planning, responding to our real needs as clearly outlined evaluation methodologies to determine effectiveness and satisfaction through annual publications.

✦ ✦ ✦

The food crisis in Haiti does not originate from our inability to produce for ourselves; it is a direct result of the hamstrung system whereby a lack of investment, farm insurance and reliable zoning and property law continue to prevent agricultural development. A self-respecting country should in no way import food it can produce for itself. Food production is more important to the nation's welfare than other business products. The government has an obligation to design a full agenda of support to sustainable agriculture through education and research, the rehabilitation of the subsidized agricultural financial system to provide loans and insurance coverage to farmers, identify lands to convert into farmlands and, more importantly, regulate and revitalize agrarian production to feed the population and supply global markets.

The government must introduce policies that integrate poverty alleviation to empower poor farmers throughout the country, promote sustainable agricultural practices that will protect the ecosystem and its ability to provide for the farmers who depend on them. We must work to turn the agriculture sector into our vehicle for sustainable development through policies that promote environmental sustainability, rural vitality and a healthy farm sector. Haiti's abundant and fertile land, cost-effective labor, accessible technology and cutting-edge chemical research in fertilizers and seeds guarantee all the

A self-respecting country should in no way import food it can produce for itself.

advantages for a competitive food producer in the Caribbean. We can promote aquaculture through vast fish-farming projects and fishing industries to fasten substantial improvement in the living conditions of the coastal rural areas, slow down the mass exodus and encourage fishermen to become contributors to the sustainability of the national economy.

Haiti's agriculture must be protected by insurance policies to cover loss of crop and livestock yield from any and all types of natural causes, including drought, excessive moisture, disease and coverage options against potential loss in revenue. Through public-private partnerships, the Ministry of Agriculture and the Ministry of Commerce can structure, regulate and authorize private companies to service delivery of mandatory and affordable agricultural insurance programs to every eligible farmer upon request. By combining the regulatory authority and financial support of the government, risk can be sustainably shared among the private companies as well as the government.

These goals of strengthening agriculture as reinforcement of our moribund national production must be appointed to a critical infrastructure of food supply chain that accurately plans and executes movement of our goods across geographic locations with speed and enhanced agility to meet local demands and reduce our dependence on imports. The safety and quality of our finished products are dependent on the integrity of the entire chain from the farm to the fork, which requires the Ministry of Public Health to regulate our warehouses, manufacturers and distribution centers, with systems and approaches in place to safeguard quality assurance.

Preservation of the environment should be the government's imperative, not only for safeguarding food production, but also protecting the air and water from contamination, sustaining livelihoods and preserving public health. The environment is our shared living space that we must constantly protect by reconstruction and beautification. Its degradation exacerbates poverty conditions for those who rely on natural resources for economic advancement. Our economic policies often ignore the contribution of such goods in our statistics. They also find it difficult to justify the urgency of this need when the benefits to responding to environmental problems accrue over time. Meanwhile, our most vulnerable, who rely mostly on the environment and have the lowest capacity to influence political process and decision-making, outside of voting, cannot express their discontent.

The government must design programs to restore a green infrastructure in an effort to rebuild the country's depleted natural resources and revitalize our landscape by planting millions of trees in forests bearing the names of our founding fathers to prevent flood and soil erosion. Moreover, we must develop new and improve existing water, sewer and storm-water systems to enable our cities and metropolitan areas to function as centers of commerce, industry, entertainment and human habitation. Water supply and basic sanitation services are still quite deficient, constituting a public health hazard; bad excreta disposal practices are polluting almost all eighteen water sources supplying Port-au-Prince. We need to establish a modern sewage system to deliver water to our major cities.

In addition to the establishment of adequate sewage systems, we must institute a fully integrated waste management and recycling infrastructure to collect waste, clean up plastic pollution and manage landfills responsibly. These measures to reverse environmental degradation have the potential to positively impact areas that have not seen much movement from one administration to the next. Improving waste management and reduction can not only solve our consumer waste crisis but also open access to a range of industries linked to recycling, which can generate considerable employment opportunities, including for skilled and semiskilled labor. This could also be an advantageous approach to establishing ecotourism, which often leads to profitable economic activities, in tandem with better access to communications and enhanced participation in global markets. Our residential areas must be livable and our tourist areas attractive, free of the sight and stench of backed-up sewers.

✦ ✦ ✦

Tourism is more than just a means to an end, a way of bringing in outside capital. It requires government partnership and a well-defined public policy to promote thriving arts, cultural scenes and entertainment reflective of Haiti's unique character, culture, historical heritage and resources. It should serve as a competitive economic engine to sustain infrastructure and suprastructure projects as determinants of development, fueling and shaping our global character.

I have traveled the world and witnessed the wonders of sustainable tourism. I have visited countries famed for the same hospitality Haiti naturally exudes. Sometimes their island chains of captivating blends of mountains, undulating, windswept dunes that merge with blue sea on unspoiled beaches and peaceful seaside villages, as in our country, leave visitors wanting more. Other times, mainlands of modern culture, skyscrapers and megastructures exhibit the far-reaching limits of human ingenuity. From the depths of their cultural authenticity and religious traditions to their natural and socioeconomic restraints, they use their opportunities to expand their tourism sector. I have read tales of patients who journey thousands of miles for specialized medical care, of students who travel to distant lands in pursuit of higher knowledge, of inquirers who visit foreign lands to develop agriculture and individuals who search the far ends of the globe for personal transformation through spiritual healing, all of which encompass activities of sustainable tourism.

Haiti has much of the same on which to capitalize: weather, geography and a tropical landscape that have turned many of our Caribbean neighbors into holiday paradises and popular tourism destinations. Forgetting our glorious culture and enriching past has impoverished us in several respects and has contributed to our continued divergence from the rest of the world. We often invoke our cultural richness and its potential, but no effort has been made to boost the tourism sector and make it economically viable. The enhancement of different facets of Haitian culture could attract visitors from around the globe, with its patrimonial portfolio comprising 114 forts, 149 historical monuments, 111 beaches, 86 archaeological sites and 76 caves, to list only a few of the attractions that once made Haiti a popular destination.

The link between tourism and the domestic economy is not yet fully developed in Haiti. It has always and continues to offer enormous opportunities for generating broad growth and economic development for the entire region. It is estimated that the tourism industry in and around the Caribbean employs one in four people directly or indirectly, is responsible for more than $2 billion in revenue per year according to the International Tourism Organization (ITA). Thus, massive investment in the tourism industry is a necessity for Haiti. In theory, and when done sensibly, tourism can dwarf international aid, curbing the problem of profiteering from our poverty. Like many countries that managed to do so before it, Haiti ought to reconstruct its tourism industry, notably sustainable tourism, to jump-start its economic development. Although often underestimated, sustainable tourism can help promote peace and stability in developing countries by providing jobs, generating income, diversifying the economy, protecting the environment and promoting cross-cultural awareness.

Tourism has been an afterthought here for far too long. While the Haitian government has been supported by the Caribbean Tourism Organization to restore the island's image as a tourist destination, the social priorities after the earthquake and subsequent disasters have forced tourism to take a back seat to the pressing needs of food and health security. Toning down the importance of the sector was understandable amid those crises. However, now there are reasons to focus on this area and to provide the means and motivation for nationals and foreigners to invest. Now is the time to create the conditions to attract foreign tourists such as security, cleanliness, social and political stability.

The key part of the word "tourism" is "tour." There must be offerings including fine restaurants, world-class hotels and art museums to accommodate visitors and dazzle them with our Haitian hospitality. Although our beaches do not yet meet international standards, the government could play an instrumental role in incentivizing local and international hospitality investors to convince luxury hotel chains to build in the coastal areas. This endeavor could bring considerable traffic to our many beaches, which would positively impact the health of local and national economies. As one of the oldest nations in the hemisphere, we need to build a tourism industry that will be one more pillar that upholds Haiti as a beacon of commerce in the Caribbean.

Government slogans are not enough to reboot tourism in Haiti. For sustainable tourism to deliver on its promises of prosperity, three main stakeholders must participate in reshaping the industry: the government, the community and foreign investors. A comprehensive plan ought to include synergy between all three parties. While the government must establish tax incentives, supportive strategies to remove bottlenecks and develop international business standards and legal framework, the communities must work to improve service delivery, protecting their environment and culture. With those parameters established, foreign investors would prioritize Haiti as a viable area for investment and procure the knowledge, technological and financial resources toward the development of the industry in the country.

When I revisited the North to recapture in detail the meanings of areas I have overlooked for years, it took me nine hours from Port-au-Prince, a distance that could have been covered in no more than three hours with a highway system less perilous. If it were not for that fact, local tourism could play a more significant role in the economic output of areas with as much significance as Cap-Haitian. They say it is a writer's compulsion to look at events, objects and even the invisible to detect in them a story as it needs to be remembered, but Cap-Haitien speaks for itself. The city's numerous historical corners and unique attractions enthralled me in a less-than-two-hour tour.

We must take both our tourism infrastructure and

suprastructure into consideration when developing systems to support tourist activities. Particular challenges are presented in developing transport systems and providing adequate accommodation in these areas, as accessibility remains the biggest impediment to visiting those places. We must institute a transportation overhaul, building a highway network and a public system to interconnect Haiti's ten geographical departments, leading to better access to our ports, airports, historical sites, caves, seaside resorts and waterfalls to enhance all areas of economic attractions.

The development of our suprastructures must also reveal our standing as the oldest nation to gain its independence in the western hemisphere. If we truly owe our independence to voodoo, it should not be inconceivable to have a mega-attraction built around the religion. I recently visited Dubai, a country that has managed to draw millions of visitors to not just one but many of its religious sites, with the Grand Mosque in Abu Dhabi representing a pillar of the United Arab Emirates' tourism industry. Europe, the Americas and Asia all utilize the same strategy of using suprastructures such as cathedrals and religious sites to attract pilgrims and spiritual seekers. Similarly, Haiti can build upon its existing resources, such as its culture of voodooism, Kanaval and Rara to draw in the tourists of the world and promote a prosperous

Haiti. We ought to build a voodoo temple on par with its contribution to our history and culture as a nation, giving visitors yet one more reason to choose the country as their vacation destination.

Kanaval remains the country's most popular festival, and has moved beyond Haiti to major cities in the United States and other countries, generating hundreds of millions of dollars. Though widely attended in our country, many of the participants are from the diaspora, returning for a chance to relax and visit their families. While the government spends a considerable amount of money organizing carnivals, it runs a deficit annually, thus confirming the assumptions that ambulatory festivities are a huge waste of money. The majority of the government funds allocated go to building stands, a temporary setup that should be permanent infrastructure. In an attempt to generate profits, the government rents out these stands, a practice that perpetuates corruption. Meanwhile, a third of Brazil's national budget comes from carnival entries. The support of the organization of the Brazilian carnival by the central state promotes these festivities in the national economic interest.

We can reduce the financial strain on the government and reposition Haiti to a lucrative design of carnival celebrations by modernizing the entire sector. We need a contemporary, permanent infrastructure, a central point of assembly capable of receiving an influx of millions of visitors to our annual carnival celebration. We can harness our folklore, Rara and culture for productive economic purposes. Our Rara can reveal mythological riches, tales and legends, adages and long-forgotten or unknown stories that could enrich the way we think of indigenous people. Haitians and foreigners alike are very keen on embracing the authentic display of our rich culture, so much so that our Rara has become a source of intrigue and inspiration for international researchers. The Raras of Léogâne, Petit-Goâve, Aquin, North-West and Artibonite are starting to attract large crowds from here and elsewhere. Therefore, it is becoming urgent and essential that we nationalize the Haitian Rara and beautify it so it is more attractive and beneficial to the country and the local economy. These walking bands enhance the country's cultural wealth by reviving our knowledge of the lives of previous civilizations, particularly their clothing, customs and traditions. Hence the need to strengthen, energize and enhance the festivities to make the Haitian Rara profitable. All of these cultural facets must be explored, exploited and sold for Haiti's benefit.

The experience of many destinations worldwide is that a planned approach to tourism development can lead to many socioeconomic benefits in the long run. The entire Caribbean is heavily dependent on tourism to sustain economic growth, with the industry accounting for 15.2 percent of regional GDP in 2017. As a result, the region's governments have worked hard to refurbish tourist facilities and infrastructure to attract millions of tourists annually. They foresee that people will want to enjoy a pleasant tourist experience in the most beautiful atmospheres again when the pandemic subsides. Haiti cannot afford not to be ready.

Like other Caribbean nations, Haiti can expect increased currency stability because tourism remains a significant source of foreign exchange earnings. Tourism would also lead to the diversification, creation and prioritization of Haitian jobs, which would result in gender equality and, ultimately, serve our women empowerment objectives. It would be unwise to dismiss the positive impact such a shift would have on the most impoverished, reducing the vulnerability of the poor. Most importantly, tourism could be a significant contributor to tax revenue that could improve infrastructure, education and health care.

Sustainable tourism can provide a positive experience for local people, tourism companies and tourists alike. In embracing the industry, the Haitian government and our people can reap the many benefits of economic development. That said, key challenges must be addressed if Haiti is to enjoy any peace-stabilizing benefits from this industry, including investments in infrastructure and human capacity, by restructuring the education system, the development of comprehensive national strategies, the adoption of robust regulatory frameworks, mechanisms to maximize in-country foreign currency earnings and efforts to reduce crime and corruption to strengthen our middle class through economic prosperity.

✦ ✦ ✦

Our education system continues to fail the majority of our youth. It leaves them without access to quality training to evolve in the global economy. The system suffers from conditions that still plague most of the countries in the "bottom billion": deficient government funding, lack of access to quality schools, few trained teachers, unavailability of learning materials, inadequate financial means, foreign language inaptitude and constant political instability. For our generation to guarantee a country with unlimited economic growth, we must start with education. This sector warrants a total reform. Haiti needs a world-class public education system that is advanced, progressive and responsive to the needs of the country—with equal access to student loans and grant programs facilitating upward mobility, job-skills training to increase marginalized groups' ability to move up in the career ladder and level the playing field.

Education remains one of the primary methods through which individuals get the preparation and qualification necessary to become valuable contributors of society. Other nations saw, centuries ago, that by investing heavily in an equal and universal education system, they were able to progress economically. Though Haiti has made dramatic efforts to increase access to education in the past two decades, challenges still exist. The education system faced tremendous trials after the earthquake and other natural disasters, including significantly diminished capacities for responding to them. The loss of good teachers, schools and administrators compounded the problems of a system already plagued with a shortage of qualified teachers, schooling infrastructure and adequate governance mechanisms. The primary concerns were then, and remain, the lack of classrooms for children to enroll in free public schools, late entry and low school progression due to the cost burden on families and the relatively low quality of education due to high demand and a proliferation of private schools. Eighty percent of Haitian schools are private. Tuition, even in the lowest-cost private schools, remains prohibitive for poor families, especially for those living in rural areas.

Haiti must swiftly embark on a complete reform of

its primary, secondary and higher education system. Our starting point should be a greater allocation of government funds to create and maintain a well-regulated public education system, complete with modern schools, providing all children with the quality education they need to succeed. But reform initiatives must also include a mass literacy campaign and job-skills training throughout the country to increase the upward mobility and economic stability of marginalized groups, correcting the errors of our past and our failure to educate more than 40 percent of our population. In this new information age driven by science, technology and an increasingly competitive global economy, the future depends, in large part, on the access to and quality of the education and skills training our people receive.

From the outset, the orientation of our public education system has not reflected the country's reality. As a relic of colonial times, we are one of the last places in the world where the legal and instructional language are different from the mother tongue. This variance represents a controlling and oppressive stratagem severing our people from the government and the institutions meant to serve them. Its effects are most apparent in the lack of analytical and logical reasoning plaguing even our most classically educated persons. If nothing else is ever accomplished in education reform in this country, let it be that all instructional education be conducted in Haitian Creole.

We also need to educate and train our people according to a clear vision, preparing them to meet the challenging needs of the country. We must strive to build analytical and logical thinkers capable of identifying, synthesizing and solving our most pressing issues, preparing all citizens adequately to maintain the pace of change in the world and undoubtedly increase our standards of living. The quality of education is highly dependent upon the caliber of our educators. We should conduct a national review and implementation of pedagogy among teachers. The current laissez-faire approach to teaching has led to wildly varying levels of education, with high divergence in learning materials. The working conditions of most teachers, their level of training and education and low remunerations are all unacceptably below international standards.

We must address these concerns with respect to their level of importance if we are to improve the quality of education. We must implement a basic national standard, adopted across both public and private schools, with applicable textbooks and curriculum. Everywhere else in the Caribbean, governments have begun to require teachers to pass tests to be certified. We can implement continuing education and mandatory certification for teachers reflective of the direction of our education system, and adopt recommendations for the gradual improvement of the quality of teaching through the Institut Pédagogique National (IPN) and the Centres Pédagogique Régional (CPR).

Our higher education system remains one of the most expensive in the Caribbean. Physical access is even more limited considering most universities are located within Port-au-Prince. These facts create more strain on families already spread thin financially. Moreover, lack of access to higher education creates an influx of students who ultimately do not contribute to the economic advancement of the country. The government must implement the disbursement of subsidies and loan programs to support students at the university level, research and continuing education in selected fields that will propel the country forward—science, technology, engineering, the arts and mathematics. The curriculum and course study for higher education should not be designed to serve students' personal aspirations alone, but communities and the country at large as the government provides schools of higher education with generous research and development subsidies in areas that will foster faster and better industrial development and promote greater self-reliance for domestic industries.

✦ ✦ ✦

Our economy needs a clear plan and steady leadership. Today, the world sees no limit to economic growth. Capital and technology give rise to all kinds of new business sectors and opportunities for employment that Haiti continues to miss out on. Our country currently has a nineteenth-century financial system consisting of two subsectors, one formal and the other informal, both largely organized primarily to supply the financial needs of the wealthy. Corruption pervades both commerce and politics, leading to our country's suppressed economic growth. We have seen a plethora of administrations inherit and leave behind a trail of inefficient management of public sector enterprises, inefficient utilization of domestic resources, lack of technological advancement, no research and development and slow innovation. Amid our cycles of political instability and natural catastrophes, we continue to endure rising fiscal deficits, mainly due to the nondevelopmental expenditures of our administrations.

We *must* do better. We *can* do better. Without a well-functioning financial system, neither foreign aid nor local entrepreneurship can create the right business conditions for long-term growth. Our priority must be to promote an appropriate economic environment, a conducive legal and regulatory framework

and the development of sustainable financial interme-
diaries in both urban and rural areas. We need to forge
an economic strategy for Haiti, an economic framework that will instill internal and external confidence
in its economy. We must introduce reforms aimed at
bringing real and sensible participation of the private
sector in the growth process of the economy at large,
and strive for improvements that span banking sector
reform, technology upgrades and foreign investments
and trade, as we promote higher rates of national production, reductions of government deficit and overcome the credit crisis.

Haiti needs strong banking reform to put an
end to the unconscionable, fraudulent and predatory practices in the financial sector. Our economic
reforms must correlate with poverty alleviation and
access to services for development and growth. We
must redesign the banking infrastructure to implement the types of credit systems that align with that
of the rest of the world so we can access outside
private capital with reliability. All citizens and businesses must have access to a fully functional national
credit system, as Banque de la République d'Haiti
ensures reasonable macroeconomic stability through
monetary policies that effectively manage inflation
and interest rates.

Economic reforms should be synonymous with

complete structural adjustments in our financial, industrial and agricultural sectors and global trade to spur growth. The restructuring of the financial system should entail a review of laws and policies that no longer correspond to the current reality. The repeal of these laws and their replacement with ones in line with the renovation of the country will equip institutions with the tools to empower investors and entrepreneurs to take full advantage of the new opportunities created. A strong financial system requires depth, access, efficiency and stability. We must unshackle our public sectors from the cobwebs of unscrupulous bureaucratic controls and increase the parameters for foreign investments, making room for entrepreneurs with the objective of integrating the Haitian economy with the world economy.

Our financial system should be focused on empowering entrepreneurial potential for growth—promote innovation and entrepreneurship through favorable tax programs, mobilize part of our gross domestic product in productive private investments to allow Haiti to obtain access to attractive markets on favorable terms, insert itself into global value chains while at the same time engaging in responsive public-private dialogue. It is time we truly promote our openness and attractiveness to direct foreign investment, opening up our borders to the multinationals to raise investments to support our high-priority industries and programs. Haiti can easily become a favorable investment destination for foreign investors. We have advantageous geography, affordable labor and an abundant workforce.

We can take measures to diffuse technology as an engine for growth, giving our youth access to a wide range of future possibilities. We can initiate a supermarket management system under municipal governments' supervision to promote upward socio-economic mobility as we regulate all trading activities to unify the informal economy with the formal structure. The key is to modernize public markets through comprehensive government programs to provide merchants with attractive, clean and secure spaces that meet international standards for the sale of national products under impeccable conditions. The end goal is to encourage the emergence of businesses of all kinds to create jobs, reducing unemployment and gradually improving the living conditions of the population as a whole. Our domestic industries can increase labor productivity, producing quality goods, thereby creating efficient companies that will compete in the global markets.

✦ ✦ ✦

The bedrock of Haiti's industrial rejuvenation is a reconstructed modern and sustainable energy system. We need major reform of the energy sector, prioritizing renewable energy through public-private partnerships to ensure substantial cost reduction in infrastructure investment, improve economic growth and strengthen competitiveness. There is no way to overstate the problems that lack of energy has brought us. Nothing that I can write in this book can bring catharsis for the pain felt by the impact of electrical disruptions and the aggravation of energy-cost fluctuations. The cost of fuel has been one of the most significant setbacks to the prosperity of Haitian families. We have experienced decades of failed national efforts to pull away from political, economic and natural catastrophes, all hampered by energy problems.

This situation must change. There is an urgent need to repair and expand existing power plants throughout the country. We are still debating our electrical problems when the world is on the cusp of significant change in the development, perception and distribution of energy. Clean energy is a smart and viable option for Haiti, a sector where we can lead the way. We not only can draw from technologies being developed around the world for renewable energy, we can draw, even today, on the minds of our young people and their ingenuity. Our rivers run with great enough force to harness nonpolluting hydraulic energy, the sun exploited for solar power stations. Some of our peaks are perfectly positioned to channel cross-Caribbean currents to power wind turbines. Geographically speaking, there is no part of Haiti that cannot in some way be utilized to produce affordable and constant energy. What we lack in traditional sources can be made up for in the country's natural landscape, drenched in sunlight 85 percent of the time. We stand at an opportune time to take advantage of innovations to rejuvenate our nation by constructing a modern energy system on a par with our aspirations.

Our entire economic vibrancy and existence relies on energy security. Almost every other month, gas shortages paralyze our economy and fuel unrests against failing leaderships and dysfunctional politics. The government must plan beyond simple electricity reform toward long-term energy security to power our economic engine at an affordable price. We can design a national plan encompassing different energy mixes to meet our national needs as we maintain regulations that provide a framework for emergency oil stockpiling. We should also create programs to overcome the barriers to adopting cleaner cooking technologies for our rural populations, with less access to cleaner fuels, who depend on cutting down trees for fuel. Lastly, a responsible government should introduce a program to monitor future energy needs to meet projected increased national transportation demands.

✦ ✦ ✦

Haiti needs a public transportation overhaul—a system designed, structured, implemented and operated with the ability to handle the flow of people and commercial goods throughout the country. We must build an eight-lane highway network to interconnect the ten geographical departments, giving better access to our ports, airports, historical sites, caves, seaside resorts and waterfalls so all areas with attractions can be reached, to improve our dysfunctional and inefficient transport conditions, alleviate public discontent and suffering and do away with critical environmental issues and bad road conditions. We need three tiers of roads in our network: interconnected, multilane highways that contribute to better logistics for agriculture and industry, bypass roads that connect our smaller towns and villages and local roads that promote commuting and business activity within every community. With this kind of network, we can decentralize the host of activities within the capital and deliver autonomy to the outskirts of our country. This should occur as part of a macroeconomic strategy conducive to fostering strong economic conditions, opening the country to global trade, creating jobs and satisfying our long-term, regional, sustainable development plans.

Our current public transportation can be characterized as a progression of disorder carried on by private providers under poorly regulated fares and routes, coupled with substandard planning, enforcement and control strategies. Weak government regulation has allowed excessive transport vehicle fleets, inadequate vehicle sizes and shapes, irregular operation and minimal vehicle and infrastructure maintenance. Pockets of all major cities suffer from high levels of congestion, motor vehicle accidents and a host of negative effects on the environment. This deterioration of the transportation system is indicative of the government's laissez-faire attitude toward policy design and its enforcement. As a result, the transit system is ill-equipped to handle the modern industrialized nation Haiti is to become.

A first-class road system can have measurable positive impacts that include a cleaner and larger public transport system to reduce congestion, travel times, air pollution and traffic-related injuries and deaths, thereby improving public health. We must institute a comprehensive strategy that combines financial, legal and environmental resources through public-private partnerships to deliver a well-regulated and efficient system with a host of buses and taxis to service the population and improve tourism. Sustainable urban transport has the potential of transforming all our departments and cities.

Our waterways can be used to expand our transit system, as well as advanced marine transportation for commercial, recreational and scientific purposes. With the private sector already owning and operating the vessels and most of the existing cargo ports and being responsible for the commerce that flows through the system, we can broaden joint private-public sector maritime enterprise options to reduce congestion and promote more economic activity.

Our transportation overhaul must incorporate a cutting-edge communication network for better Internet connectivity, information sharing and communication technology services to promote economic growth, improve our politics, advance medicine and influence culture. Communication is key. The Conseil National des Télécommunications (CONATEL), the regulatory body for telecommunications services in the country, should be modernized to increase its efficiency in assuring the quality of the services offered by all providers. The institution's past refusal, whether because of corruption or lack of foresight, to fully liberalize the telecommunications market slowed investments that would bring new jobs, capital and infrastructure, all of them needed to stimulate the growth of the gross domestic product. Countries in our region that understood this fact ahead of others have been able to diversify their economies and empower their citizens by not relying solely on their primary industries, like agriculture and fishing.

We need to harness a dedication to technology with a stronger connection to the people. The Internet will certainly be a battleground in the next presidential elections. CONATEL must provide government solutions to implement public-private synergies that allow the country to truly enter the technology age. The council must also look into options for national policy to fully liberalize the market, promoting competition and a rapid growth in services, but, most importantly, to develop and modernize the country. Improving our way of life is dependent on rapid growth and technical advancements. Let that be our future.

TRANSPARENCY
AND
ACCOUNTABILITY

*A new government standing on three foundational
pillars: transparency, accountability and strength.*

I N THE BEGINNING of January 2020, nations around the world began to take appropriate measures to deal with the coronavirus outbreak. The pandemic forced world governments better equipped and more informed than Haiti to their knees, implementing curfews and confinements, stock market shutdowns, border closings and mass testing to curb the spread of the virus. A looming fear hung over Haiti. Chronic underfunding of public health, an inefficient health-care system and inadequate testing measures would neuter the nation's ability to accurately count our sick citizens and prevent the pathogen from gaining a foothold. Despite ample warning and having had enough time to pay attention to other nation's preparedness and adapt a proper plan for our nation, our government officials careened between inaction and ineptitude. Three months later, in mid-March, President Moïse addressed the nation, declaring a state of emergency. It was clearly a sluggish response by a government denuded of expertise. The statement left a population that was already frantic with more questions than answers, in complete disarray.

In times of catastrophe, be it a pandemic, rising unemployment, food scarcity or natural disaster, a people always look to its government for solutions. But our country's institutional deficit has long affected the people's perception of government. The weaknesses that have kept the government from effectively addressing our economic hardship have been the biggest impediment to the country's social stability. Each time the country began to recover from its long, brutal history of colonialism and ruthless dictatorships, the elite and foreign sponsors that developed vested interests in the chaos would work to maintain the status quo so they continue to profit from the weakness of our government. This phenomenon has only left room for predatory globalization policies, marginal taxes on incomes or low tariffs on imports, negligible national regulations, a lack of social justice or minimal interference in the exploitation of labor, trade deficit or contraband that have been impeding on our opportunities to build the necessary infrastructure required to progress on our terms.

Only a strong national government that has operational authority and the structure to use its power to impact localities everywhere can organize Haiti's renewal. This national government's role will be to regain control of our basic industrial and socioeconomic projects from the politically ambitious who continue to use them as electoral bargaining chips; a government that favors seamless transitions between administrations, in the form of permanent layers whose sole purpose is to maintain continuity of basic systems and removing them from the control of one political entity or another. This will culminate in a functioning government able to exercise strength and integrity beyond just the security apparatus, but in justice, taxation, education and socioeconomic development.

This idea of a strong government should not suggest the duplication of the abuses of the past. The cruelties of dictatorship and misapplications of democracy should no longer be tolerated. We must band together to form a government of the people and for the people, and participate in the country's rejuvenation. The politicians of this new era are to be true public servants operating according to our will. It will no longer be in their power to undermine government systems, put up walls or utilize the state as their own private entity. This new government must stand on transparency, accountability and strength as the three foundational pillars that allow for change along a path of continuous growth for the nation.

Transparency must complement strong authority for government to exercise its power legitimately, a condition of openness as a prerequisite to effective governance. The country's future lies in its ability to conjure its people into participation from the bottom up to create a responsive state centered on accelerating the deployment of change to improve quality of life. Transparency breeds informed constituency and informed voters are key to effective decision-making. A transparent government that publishes its facts and figures, its revenue and tax streams, its laws and policies, which can be held accountable and deemed trustworthy. By providing citizens with a window into the state's actions, we are enabling healthier public debate and political participation, an essential driver of economic growth and social development.

Fiscal transparency can be achieved by combining clarity in spending with openness in other government areas, including implementing policies and regulations that will allow the people to see the full extent of their government's financial resources and the impact of their policies on public finances. In other words, the public must see how money is being allocated and how it is being spent. The two are not always interchangeable. Although recent improvements have been made to increase transparency, the lack thereof has, in the past, rendered international investors hesitant to invest in sustainable projects in Haiti.

We must continue to improve upon our efforts to be more transparent by implementing annual reviews of fiscal reports to provide an opportunity for dialogue and to assess areas for improvement. The bidding and planning stages pertaining to government contracts should be open to public scrutiny. Government websites should publish contract procedures, the criteria for contract awards, the contracts' scope, requirements and time frames. Budget documents should be made available to the public and should provide detailed information on actual expenditures and tax revenues at the very least. This process already dominates government and business partnerships all over the world because moving from one government project to the next can be wasteful. Too many administrations have allocated and disbursed funds to pet projects they knew would end at the eve of a new administration. This practice must cease; government spending should be tied to well-defined metrics assessing both effectiveness and efficiency over the long haul, to improve the quality of our economy and democracy.

This segment of my narrative would not be complete without a mention of the press, which plays a part in promoting transparency, providing the people with information, holding elected officials accountable and eventually, perhaps, shaping opposition to the government. But sometimes the implications of media misinformation has proven dire for Haiti. The lack of trust in a government known mostly for its abuse and neglect has rendered efforts to dispel common misinformation ineffective. Where the people would otherwise turn to trusted government media outlets for public announcements, they may turn to extremists and conspiracy theorists, media personalities of stubborn mindset who provide the country with ideas and views, political thoughts and opinions with which to challenge the establishment.

For many years the press has deliberately bombarded the people of Haiti with mendacious and incendiary remarks, creating the perfect vacuum for political instability, which a select few continue to exploit for their own wealth and power. The result was a preoccupied constituency, a deactivated people, a nation slumped in apathy and conceit, too concerned with finding their daily bread to confront its collective problems, becoming a breeding ground for dysfunction.

In the end, for individuals like me, who submit our will and dreams of building a better Haiti, the desire to remain well informed on social issues is constantly at odds with the need to remain sane. Every day brings a theater of escalating rhetoric between the press and the government. They partner with agitators and ensure that every single movement, every right, every cause have momentum. Much as in some other nations, we have been dealing with the effects of uncensored speech. While other governments have enacted policies and ethical rules to curb the practice, ours has made little effort to repress false reporting. We ought to change the environment and the impact of misinformation on our public safety and public order. When the role of traditional media seems inconspicuous, technology remains one of the driving forces impacting participation in most working democracies. Social media can be instrumental in disseminating accurate information when needed and in raising awareness in times of catastrophe.

While other countries have approached their people and re-engaged their citizenry, our officials have done little to nothing to rebuild trust. Too many profit from the lack thereof. This fragmented relationship between elected officials and their role to serve the nation's interest came into question once again when the rapper Kanye West announced details about his meeting with the Moïse administration. During an interview, he alluded that the government had given him La Gônave island to develop. If true, this would mean that the administration made a unilateral decision without involving or informing the public about the nature and terms of the deal. Most people learned of the negotiations after they had taken place. This type of decision-making continues to promulgate the same disappointments echoed about previous administrations.

Citizens must have access to the accurate, substantive and truthful information they need to hold their government accountable. We deserve full transparency about decisions that impact our lives and must have a voice in the matters. Our nation is still enduring the repercussions of unilateral decisions made by previous administrations. Wisdom should caution us from stumbling into the same pitfalls. We must build on high ethical standards and solid technological foundations to develop an efficient information ecosystem, not only to enable the public to gauge the effectiveness and efficiency of the government's decisions, but also to provide access for their direct or indirect participation and contribution. The time has come for the people and private industries to be empowered by a transparent, accountable and strong government underpinning economic sustainability, help promote confidence in private markets and guarantee a society of peace, security and prosperity.

✦ ✦ ✦

Haiti must regain greater control of revenue streams to finance its effectiveness and strength, through the innovation of the process through which the DGI collects income taxes, the transformation of Customs and the Authorité Portuaire Nationale (APN), the total reform of the national lottery system, the creation of a national circulation center and reforming the Office d'Assurance Vehicules Contre Tiers (OAVCT). Our inability to manage our own revenue streams has created a recurring cycle of dependence on foreign and humanitarian aid. A sovereign nation must provide for its people. The first legitimate power of government is the authority to impose and collect taxes. Reorganizing our streams and taking fiscal responsibility represents the first step toward providing for the country. The government's capacity to collect its due must expand to produce better tax revenues to fulfill its sovereign mission, to reinforce, to revitalize our public institutions.

Inconsistent records and poor tax collection efforts can no longer characterize the way the DGI addresses state revenues. The institution needs an unprecedented reorganization and modernization to render its services swift, effective and satisfactory, thereby eliminating endless discontent. The modernization of the institutions' processes and practices should help collect more money in taxes and restructure a system that monitors earnings and puts business and people in control of their tax information—giving them a clear understanding of their tax burden.

For its part, the government must introduce a comprehensive fiscal policy overhaul, criminalizing tax evasion and oriented toward more progressive objectives, sustaining inclusive growth. When we consider the rates applied to each bracket, a heavier burden weighs on the middle class, and current taxation fails to seize important resources on higher levels of income. We could exponentially grow revenue and expand our tax base by simply modifying the rate for the personal income tax. We must also close the loopholes in the tax administration and collection process. The country needs a taxation structure that reflects its underlying socioeconomic makeup. Simultaneously, the government must integrate an efficient system with the latest technology to position the DGI at an advantage to both levy and collect taxes, as we publish valuable resources to help people understand how the change impacts their lives, their communities and the national economy.

The bulk of our taxation revenue comes from international transactions on imports. We need updating technology and management systems at the APN to curb corruption, facilitate better tariff collection and provide greater financial prospects. Modernization should facilitate rapid customer service, promote increases in revenue and effectively control customs services. Modifications could be made to streamline customs exemptions granted on imports and increase revenues. But we must properly study and analyze fiscal policies for rationalizing exemptions except for nongovernment organizations and diplomatic missions operating within the boundaries set by international treaties, and in ways that ensure satisfactory revenue gains without dampening the profitability of businesses or discouraging donors.

The government and the Loterie de l'État Haitien (LEH) must fully appropriate gambling to dismantle organized crime and secure a substantial stream of revenue aimed at financing projects of national interest, such as education and social programs, without raising taxes. A select few independent firms regrouped under the Association Nationale des Tenanciers de Borlette (ANTB) have been running the gambling industry for decades, reaping millions in profits while the government gains almost nothing from these vast flows of cash. Out of nearly 400,000 gambling stations, called borlettes, only 30 percent regularly pay the taxes due to LEH. The estimated shortfall costs the state about four or five billion gourdes every year. Through defining a new legal framework, we can equip the lottery commission with the modern technology necessary for a sound and rigorous management of the industry to increase prizes and the number of winners, so that more people have a positive experience.

The lack of traffic enforcement is another crippling factor in the government's low-revenue generation for the treasury. The absence of law enforcement, traffic signals, signs and pavement markings, street identifications and vehicle inspections renders our streets very dangerous. Too many drivers repeatedly violate the traffic laws and exhibit aggressive and illegal behaviors on public roads, endangering lives and private properties. The government must create a national circulation center, with decentralized services to localities, tasked with administering vehicle registration and driver licensing, making sure that all owners of vehicles with valid registrations comply with the laws of insurance requirements.

Technology is constantly evolving, including available traffic technology. The center should be fully equipped with cutting-edge information systems to keep track of parking tickets, moving violations, driver profiles and payments. The data can be mined not only to improve government core operations but to present entirely new regulations. It can also enable new ways to provide traditional coverage and underwrite outdated risks, often by using individual rather than group data.

The government must undoubtedly modernize the services of the OAVCT to satisfy our desire for low-cost, transparent, high-quality digital services, curbing fraud and corruption. The existing pool of vehicles across the country can be a significant revenue source for Haiti. Taxation, registrations, license plates, mandatory insurance coverage and other fees collected from the estimated 300,000 vehicles and over 500,000 motorcycles can significantly contribute to the national economy. We must innovate the operational and structural laws governing insurance service regulations. The real-time data being generated in a connected world should compel the state to adopt new practices that can help consumers mitigate risk rather than simply protect against it. Service industries that will stand out are the ones that find ways to move at the pace of a thriving economy.

The government should, both in terms of policy and technology, improve and enforce traffic laws to raise significant revenue from citations. The courts would benefit from traffic ticket revenue to pay the salaries of court personnel, including judges and lawyers. Our police officers will exercise strict control over traffic regulations across the country. The condition of vehicles in circulation will thus meet the relevant standards. The vehicle inspection service will be more efficient, with all vehicles undergoing regular inspections. Stickers will be issued to denote current inspection status. Licenses will be obtained through tests, adhering to international standards. Unruly and sanctioned drivers will find themselves restricted from the roads. We will see a dramatic reduction in accidents as we increase efforts to enforce driving regulations.

✦ ✦ ✦

Haiti needs a military structure that is compact, modern and efficient to service our borders and meet our geopolitical realities in all domains: air, land, seas, space and cyberspace. Rebuilding the new, modern armed forces of Haiti will require a well-defined conceptualization of our national realities, aligned with our foreign policy. It must not be predicated on massive investments in weapons platforms to exert national political leadership or worsen our vulnerability to military personalities, who often shaped the nation into an authoritarian and coercive style of governance in the past. We must establish a true apolitical military force, manifested in its organization, training, equipment and efficiency.

We must also rethink our existing intelligence services. The five independent intelligence operations (National Palace's intelligence, Primature's intelligence, Army's intelligence, Police Nationale's intelligence, and Ministère de l'Interieur's intelligence) responsible for the collection, analysis and exploitation of information have done a poor job of protecting the nation's secrets. They have been more successful at requesting sizable sums of taxpayers' money from the state coffers in the name of national security. Yet insecurity and instability have remained rampant for the past thirty years. Haiti needs one principal government agency to provide intelligence to the president and select cabinet members. Its establishment must adhere to constitutional principles of democracy, the rule of law and the civil and political rights of our citizens. It must be a highly efficient institution that combines military, diplomatic, economic, scientific and political operations to support our law enforcement, national security and foreign policy objectives.

Our immigration and border policy must match our national security objectives as we consider the country's circumstances, including its geography, economy and politics. The government must develop a clear-eyed view of the threats we face and the instruments necessary to defend our vital interests. Our security must be guaranteed through a sensible application of the many instruments in our power, prudence and permanent alliances with our neighbors and friendly nations. We must remain united to collectively defenestrate the incendiary comments of other nations meant to obstruct our undivided pride. Foreign affairs compel more reason and less emotion.

Our responses to verbal assaults and derogatory statements should never be undetermined or withdrawn in the silence of time. We must loudly respond to the demagogues who insist there is a "Haitian problem," as certain Dominican officials put it. And absolutely no, we are not a "shithole" country as President Trump allegedly declared. The world, as we know it, has subscribed to a more global and complex functioning unit. Haiti shares the same challenges as everywhere else in the fight against corruption, environmental issues, bad governance, natural disasters and economic issues. Nonetheless, it is my fundamental belief that the solutions to our setbacks remain Haitians' obligations only.

In that same mindset, I must respectfully submit that the Dominican Republic reserves the right to maintain its immigration strategies so long as its policies do not violate international human rights mandates and World Trade Organization rules. The systematic stripping of people into statelessness to provide an abusable labor pool is not among those standards. Such actions against its citizens of Haitian descent and the growing hostility only serve to weaken the island as a whole. Haiti and the Dominican Republic share more than an island; we share a long history anchored in collective pain, suffering and triumph. As such, we should always be able to find sustainable solutions through cooperation.

The Haitian Constitution stipulates who is considered a Haitian citizen and gives all its citizens full right to return home. This fact offers the highest legal ground possible for a repatriation program for those stripped of statehood over the border. In this instance, should the return of our compatriots need to happen, it should be done in a strategic way following open conversations between the governments of both countries. This would ensure continued respect between neighbors, promote balanced trade, economic growth and diplomatic and cultural exchanges and the pursuit of peaceful coexistence.

Nonetheless, in the interest of its national security, Haiti too has the right to regain and maintain full control of its borders to curb contraband and smuggling, which deprives the state of significant revenue, threatens national production, domestic industries and the national economy and perpetuates poverty. The government must introduce well-defined and comprehensive immigration and fiscal policies to address the trade deficit between Haiti and the Dominican Republic. Our neighbor has taken advantage of the absence of a robust Haitian regulatory system to flood our borders with smuggled goods and other illegal activities that weaken the rule of law and rob the state of vital revenues. The money our country loses because of this is equivalent to more than half of $950 million in exports. Simultaneously, the Dominican Republic's turnover in our markets is around $2 billion a year because it refuses imports from Haitian factories, even those producing at international standard.

Haiti must be able to control all the goods entering its territory through any point. We must rehabilitate, modernize and increase the number of authorized crossing points on the border and their infrastructure to promote rigorous control and better taxation revenue to the country's benefit. These positions must function twenty-four hours a day, seven days a week, supervised by highly trained customs agents. We can make better use of technology to crack down on funnel roads. Our trade policy must consider market needs and protect not only consumers but also local producers and national economic interests. The Dominican Republic must be brought back to the table for discussion to redesign sustainable trade agreements that serve the interests of both nations.

Any efforts to secure our borders without equivalent determinations into ensuring public safety within national territories will be futile. For our country to move forward and truly attain ambitious social development, economic vitality and effective governance, public security must be guaranteed. Our current lack of public safety leads to political instability and social deviancy. A functioning, professional Police Nationale d'Haiti (PNH) is a prerequisite. We must rebuild the PNH's operational capacities and clarify critical aspects of its administrative structure. Parallel to these efforts is an obligation to reinforce police capacity in our national budget. Our police need adequate funding for proper asset management, better pay, personnel supervision and leadership, and they must be able to attract the most qualified candidates.

Police development must begin with reenforcing ethics and discipline within the force at two levels. Officers who have been accused of abusing their power should be suspended immediately until their cases are resolved. Community policing is an area of reform that has not been systematically addressed. A new policing culture will see an array of men and women taking on the responsibility of protecting our communities. Stronger emphasis is needed on encouraging more women to serve in the national police. The force will train them to properly fulfill the mission of securing the country from end to end and establishing a reliable rule of law.

JUSTICE

A free, just and peaceful country maintained by a Constitution elastic enough to accommodate our collective ambitions.

THE STATE OF justice in Haiti is depressingly imbued with impossibilities. Our legal system's atrophy is blatant for everyone to witness; the evidence is all around us. The lack of justice is displayed in the decay of our abandoned buildings and unfinished construction projects, on our public sidewalks invaded with vendors, our unsafe roads with little or no traffic enforcement. Our injustice is exposed in the vacant expressions on the faces of children we have forsaken in our streets, in the way culprits with money and power flaunt the rulings of judges. It is in the characters of the politicians we elect, our weak state capacity, our underfunded health and education systems, our social disparities, our economic stagnation, and our poverty. It is unconcealed in the lack of funding in the national police force and the judiciary branch, the poor working conditions of our judges, the increasing number of unresolved legal dockets, the deprived facilities housing our courts, the flagrant human rights violations against our inmates, the blatant government interference in judicial proceedings.

In recent years, our broken justice system's effects have been manifested in the open aggressions of the gangs in our streets, who have infiltrated our collective moral fiber, rendering us immune to human reactions from criminal acts; we simply keep moving. The country is plagued by violent crimes: murders, kidnappings, carjackings and pervasive violence from conflicts between law enforcement authorities and gangs. The insecurity has affected journalists, judges, lawyers, human rights defenders and our most vulnerable groups, children and women. Many quarters in the Port-au-Prince area have become hot zones of survival of the fittest in the most deplorable forms. The people continue to face severe threats to their lives and personal security due to the proliferation of illegal arms and the government's inability to be present in many parts of the country. Law enforcement and the Haitian national police surrendered to the will of our injustice, suffering from inadequate staffing and resources, a significant deficit in morale, a lack of proper screening and training programs and an unenforced hierarchy of command. Also, instances of corruption and human rights abuses in the police force itself, the understandable lack of effective investigations and prosecutions of those perpetrators have severely tainted the institution. In the end, even the chief of police requires bodyguards to move about safely in the streets.

Inadequacies in the court system, outdated laws and law enforcement's failure to execute court orders have generated recurring delays in processing cases. The lack of access to legal assistance has resulted in a pervasive problem of prolonged pretrial delays, culminating in an increasing number of prisoners who have yet to stand trial. These deficiencies have also damaged the justice system's ability to effectively ensure and protect the unalienable rights and freedoms to which we are entitled, resulting in patterns of impunity. The working conditions for judges at all levels are unacceptable; they experience shortages of essential resources and court facilities, lack proper training and have insufficient security. Further, the judiciary's independence continues to be imperiled by such factors as the lack of security of tenure, alleged meddling in the assignment of court cases by the executive branch and the absence of a proper and functioning oversight mechanism.

Property rights remain the most pressing problem facing civil courts; our property laws are two and a half centuries of a mishmash of indecipherable complexity. Extraordinarily, little exists in the way of paper deeds that have been filed with local government.

Members of the diaspora are not spared, suffering much injustice from this land vagrancy phenomenon. The difficulties of securing one's legal property rights are first on a long list of concerns that discourage the Haitian diaspora from returning and investing their time and money in the country's future. Due to their absence from the country, the authenticity of land acquisitions by members of the diaspora is frequently contested. The irregularities in the disposition of property claims also prevent Haitians living in Haiti from acquiring land. New landowners can find themselves, to their astonishment, dispossessed by someone, or a group, claiming property rights. At the very least, new buyers must assume the expense of a risky legal battle within a vastly underfunded and often corrupt judicial system.

The national government has limited powers to expropriate property for public purposes, such as housing developments. Attempts to correct the problem have been weak, and the lack of cultural and legal respect for the diaspora remains an obstacle to economic growth and development. This lack of authority on eminent domain is a problem that needs to be solved if we want to correct the delay in our economic improvement. The underlying premise is that resolving the landownership matter is crucial to economic growth and essential to eradicating poverty, improving educational opportunities, ensuring public health and expanding infrastructure. Moreover, the lack of legal recourse and guaranteed sets of business standards for investors, including those in the diaspora, lead them to shy away from investing in the country altogether. In these circumstances, the only source of capital formation is governmental or charitable organizations. By extending legal recourse to Haitian and foreign investors, the government will give confidence in resolving modern trade disputes and attracting substantial private investment.

Corruption and its impunity remain two of the biggest stumbling blocks in our goal to boost our economic standing in the world; they impede investment, with consequent effects on growth and job creations. They have long eroded trust in revolving administrations and government, undermining our social contract, perpetuating the inequalities and discontent that lead to social violence and recurring conflicts. In casting a cleansing light and confronting these injustices, we ought to use our human and financial resources more efficiently if we hope to attract more investment, leading to rapid growth. To make inroads against corruption, the government must deploy determined efforts to overcome vested interests. While transparency and open governance can prove useful in this fight, they often are insufficient; when public discontent with corruption and cronyism reaches its peak, the political rewards to addressing corruption can exceed the costs of upsetting interests. Progress toward eradicating corruption can be achieved through better and more open processes, professional accountability systems and the use of the most advanced technologies to capture, analyze and share data to prevent, detect and deter corrupt behavior.

We must build capable and accountable institutions, and design and implement anticorruption programs relying on the latest discourse, technology and legislation. We must activate public and private actors to establish the competencies needed to implement practices that show results and strengthen public integrity. The government must rely on the judiciary as well as civil society to support efforts to prevent corruption, improve remedies to address wrongdoing while working to improve the behaviors, norms and standards needed to sustain anticorruption efforts. For our people to be enfranchised in the collective future of the nation, we must organize ourselves and our government to introduce the corrupt to justice. This will, of course, be unfavorable for those benefiting from the cloak under which our institutions operate, but the strength of our government will empower our people by removing the poor policy culture and compromised government that allows impunity to flourish.

The national consensus places the 1987 Constitution at the center of our judicial paralysis, a source of conflict spreading dysfunction through the system. Like our previous constitutions, the current one was created to omit key actors from the political process. It represents, at best, an emotional response written and ratified against the trauma of dictatorship. It contains serious flaws that have undermined the branches' ability to govern. There exists a severe disproportion between the powers the Constitution assigned to the branches of government. As it starves the judiciary of any substantial authority, it curbs executive powers by splitting the functions between a president and a prime minister. Simultaneously, it consolidates control to the legislative branch, breeding a culture of corruption and ensuring the permanence of intergovernmental conflict and gridlock. The ambiguity of its various clauses, the oversights and important gaps and the high number of elections the Constitution imposes have contributed to political instability. The document not only suffers from a lack of implementation but appears unjust from inception. The current administration knows too well the unfairness as elucidated within the Constitution. It stipulates the presidential term as five years, all the while mandating how one can lose from it. The extensive civil liberties, human rights guarantees and the number of social commitments contained therein made for an ambitious record. However, our weak state capacity combined with the lack of political will never allow any government to honor the Constitution's prescriptions, thus causing further attrition to its legitimacy.

Regardless of the turmoil that we face as a nation, the proper administration of justice must always be guaranteed. It is the government's responsibility to maintain public order, to protect our lives in a fashion consistent with the rights guaranteed by the Constitution and all other international accords Haiti observes. With justice being the bedrock of a republic, no democracy is sustainable without a well-functioning, independent judiciary that promotes public confidence in the rule of law and security. Haiti needs a constitutional reform based on four strong pillars— *Human Rights and Civil Liberties, Symmetry of Power or State Duties, Elections* and *Diaspora Integration*—a Constitution that reflects our ultimate aspirations and fulfills the dreams of future generations.

Our new or reformed Constitution must be a testament of a new and better social contract with which we can combine idealism with realism to provide a charter elastic enough to accommodate our collective ambitions and those of future generations.

We must narrate an inclusive document with authority and attribution of sound political rights and civil liberties, a document that empowers us to defend said rights and provides reliable and fair solutions to our legal impairments. The nation's cultural and socioeconomic needs should allow for a form of government that encourages our pursuit of satisfaction, provided that, in so doing, we do not infringe on the rights of others. If we are to maintain our vision of a free, just and peaceful country, human rights laws that outline practical standards for the way the government and its institutions ought to treat us should be at the core of our constitutional reform.

Our proposed amendments should provide the scope for good and effective government, achieve greater symmetry and coequality between the three branches and carry out the checks and balances necessary to secure the nation from both internal and external threats. Though the expectations are likely to differ in practice, in theory, our determination should be to prevent the risk of tyranny through a strong separation of powers that makes it impossible for one single body to exercise too much power. In that spirit, we need a bicameral legislative branch with the fundamental functions to enact the nation's laws, raise and appropriate funds, confirm or reject presidential appointments and provide for substantial investigative and impeachment powers over the executive branch.

We should also provide constitutional language that reduces the current sum of representatives to a more reasonable number as we strive to keep this legislative division as the beating heart of our democracy. All these ideas of a modern legislature should be settled in the Constitution through prescriptions that make the lawmaking function of both chambers stronger, balanced and harmonious in executive relations, a Parliamentary branch as a temple of democracy that can overcome the deep partisan divides to pass landmark legislation that continues to shape a better Haiti.

The case has already been made for a strong government and exemplary leadership to carry our progress forward. The formal constitutional responsibilities and prerogatives we vest in the executive branch should likewise affirm a strong government. As head of state and commander in chief of the armed forces, the president must be empowered to represent the nation's best interests, carry out and enforce our laws, ensure the wholesome functioning of public institutions and the continuity of the state through clear succession laws. The president should be able to nominate cabinet officials to serve at his pleasure, appoint our judges and ambassadors, negotiate treaties on our behalf.

The semipresidential system imposed by the 1987

Constitution is not compatible with our political heritage and culture. When an elected president with limited powers and a presidentially appointed prime minister chosen and functioning on the basis of parliamentary confidence, it is simply a recipe for an unproductive executive. We must replace the semipresidential system with a more functioning model that delivers both the stability and the accountability of the executive branch. In the constitutional design of this new government system, we must avoid rules that make it too easy or too difficult for Parliament to remove a government.

The long-standing intuition behind term limits was noble to an extent; we had to limit the dictatorial propensities of the past. But limiting the president's time in office to two nonconsecutive terms has only exacerbated our socioeconomic problems and hampered our government's stability. The incessant harboring of a lame-duck president has rendered Parliament inadvertently too dominant. In order to promote consistency in governance and support an environment conducive to long-term planning for our country, the new Constitution should, at the very least, provide provisions that allow a president to have two consecutive terms. The president's inherent constitutional powers should henceforth make it aberrant to maintain that he or she is a minor in the affairs of the Republic. The executive and legislative must truly be coequal branches of government. Just as the legislative can police the powers of the executive, the presidency must have the constitutional ability to veto laws from Parliament; an imbalance in favor of one branch is no better than a disproportion in favor of the other.

The judicial branch's primary functions should be the review of our laws and the oversight of our public institutions. Our Constitution should provide clear instructions about whether and how to intervene in the affairs of the other branches of government. Our reform must not only strengthen our democracy but substantially improve the justice system, promoting the rule of law. Thus, our Constitution's first moral command is to place no one above the law, not even the highest public officials. Government representatives who commit crimes or abuse the power of their office must be impeached, prosecuted and punished to the fullest extent of the law. Justice that cannot be applied, much less applied equally, is not justice at all. This understanding of the judicial process should improve the role of the courts in disciplining official misconduct, without relying on the judiciary to run the government or misusing their authority to undercut democratic accountability.

Though the Constitution's objective should be

to establish justice, it provides only the framework. There must be a supplemental and substantial change in our justice system ranging from access to quality. Our justice must embody procedural fairness, equal access and equitable application of the law, transparency in the judicial process and, most importantly, an educated and professional judicial personnel, because the quality of our justice is highly dependent on the caliber of our judges. They should be appointed based on objective criteria: experience, professionalism and reputation in the legal community, exhibiting proper judicial temperament, including courage, firmness and impartiality. These qualities should be our rational and effective nomination or appointment procedure to align with our objective of establishing a fair justice system.

We must enact into law a code of ethics for judges and an independent judicial council to enforce its provisions against corrupt judges. The rules are based on the understanding that judges must respect and honor their offices with the public's confidence and must strive to maintain and strengthen the judicial system's spirit. Irresponsible or inappropriate conduct by judges undermines public confidence in our system of justice. Judges must respect and abide by the law and act in a way that fosters public confidence in its integrity and impartiality, both within and outside the judiciary. Judges should respect and abide by the law and behave in a way that promotes public confidence in the justice system; therefore, judges must accept that their behavior outside the courthouse will be interpreted to indicate their actions inside it. The prohibitions on misbehaving apply to judges and all other court officers' professional and personal conduct.

A supervisory body, consisting of judges who rotate in their posts, must be created to check judges' conduct and ensure that they comply with the law and a judicial code of ethics. This board would be responsible for reviewing complaints of misconduct, obstruction of justice or interference in a judge's duties. Lastly, we must improve the working conditions for judges, prosecutors, clerks and bailiffs. Our judges, already underpaid, sometimes go months without pay, an indefensible situation that motivates them to seek other income streams, though they are legally barred from doing so. They often fall prey to politicians, who habitually seek to influence judicial decisions, using the system to target political opponents, culminating in a likely entry point to corruption.

Our courthouses must reflect the deference due to a great justice system; their quality should indicate the justice they dispense. Public confidence plays a major role in increasing physical access to justice. We must also decentralize some responsibilities from the national government to local authorities to reduce bottlenecks in decision-making, which often causes problems such as lack of access to resources, poor governance, poor resource management and lack of resources to enforce judgments. An independent judiciary with accessible local tribunals is essential to justice to promote legal awareness and provide accessible dispute resolution. It can also help mitigate complex bureaucratic procedures and create geographical priorities that coordinate efficiently, providing a solution to the lack of coordination between local and national governments.

We ought to create and establish legal assistance and judicial complaints offices in each municipality to respond to civil and criminal complaints and offer access to justice to those who cannot attain justice due to financial barriers. Along with these significant reforms, we must create a special housing court to fast-track and streamline land/property disputes. And we must make sure that adequate funding and authority are in place to grant courts the ability to enforce judgments, manage and administer the courts efficiently, establish satisfactory compensation for judges and staff and protect judges and witnesses from violence. This is how we may create a more functional, trustworthy justice system, one that can be expected to provide fairness, be capable of empowering a web of law enforcement institutions to fight corruption and promote public safety, a well-supervised and rich ecosystem of financial institutions and instruments and uphold the rule of law for a society of peace, security and prosperity.

Our new Constitution must address the injustices and the lack of trust in our electoral process. More than thirty years after the enactment of the 1987 Constitution, we still have not transitioned to the permanent election council it mandates. This has constituted a permanent obstacle and has negatively influenced the behavior of political actors during elections. While an independent and credible election administration is not sufficient on its own merits to assure electoral honesty, it is an essential element. Haiti needs a permanent electoral council to capitalize on the opportunities to improve and modernize our voting systems. We must ensure the electoral council members' accountability as we secure for them immunity from harassment and enable them to carry out their work impartially, professionally and without fear or favor, and to resist political pressure. The integrity of our elections is important to all of us and should be a point of shared pride. It is possible to recover public confidence in our elections. We must present fundamental reforms to put in place a stable and nonpartisan, permanent electoral council that is free of contested electoral results for decades. The new Constitution must blaringly and unequivocally dictate the mechanics of our elections with built-in features that make them highly resilient to foreign influences and domestic assaults.

Many world nations are allowing their diaspora to participate in their electoral process by recognizing dual citizenship. They do not strip people of their status if they acquire nationality in another state. In our case, the measurable increase in our community's size abroad stretched into a geopolitical space that gives more legitimacy to demands for greater political rights and representation. In the full name of justice, and to terminate the isolation era of our brothers and sisters living abroad, we must secure constitutional provisions that guarantee the diaspora's full integration in all matters relating to the country. Not only should the diaspora have the right to vote, they should be able to present themselves as candidates for all elected positions and should also relish a legal system designed to represent them in Parliament.

The right to vote and to be a candidate in elections is not meant to transform all members of the diaspora into political actors, but to strengthen our democracy and support our collective destiny by means of a planned and systematic process through which they are made a vital element of the socioeconomic and political life of Haiti as electable citizens rather than mere voters. Our road to full-scale economic development requires a critical mass of highly skilled human capital, poised to create the capacity for homeland growth and development. The promotion of such activities will allow for a diaspora that is fully engaged in Haiti's economic growth and development, a full-time commitment rather than a mere part-time, charitable one.

CONCLUSION

There is a brand-new Haiti on its way—one that can no longer be impeded by human agendas or threatened by the uncontrollable forces of nature. This new era of greatness will be ushered in as a result of all forces harmonizing toward achieving one objective: to overturn the challenges that have plagued the country for decades.

Throughout these pages, I have offered a range of thoughts and ideas that are intended to chart the course of this new era and provide cogent solutions to our past and current problems. These thoughts, greatly inspired by my family and my life experiences, redefine the formula for our success with the people at the epicenter of my dream: an experiment that will lead generations of Haitians to a dream of boundless realities—a country dedicated to the mighty proposition that *united, we are stronger.*

I believe that, working together as a powerful, united country, we can rebuild our national infrastructure, reform our energy sector, improve our education system, promote our tourism industry and overhaul our justice system. We deserve a stronger government, a vibrant economy and a more equitable society befitting of a working democracy.

Based on our nation's most recent history—born of a series of unscrupulous leaders, bad governance and lack of transparency or legal recourse—I readily empathize with those people who might initially be skeptical of Haiti's eventual change. The entering of a new administration always appears to usher in a credible prospect that all emerging demands and political disasters are behind us and that a permanent turning point has arrived. Instead, we find ourselves facing the all-too-possible prospect of our own demise.

Meanwhile, our population is tinged with contempt for a broken system; anger and despair surrounding the state of affairs has shredded political involvement, allegiance to a government meant to serve and even trust in one another. This has led to a dire erosion of confidence in the prospect of our collective survival. Many still prefer to see a sunless future facing us as they cling to our history for glorious achievements. But I ardently maintain that Haiti's brightest days lie ahead, and that if the only glories available to this nation are in its past, we must create fresh ones.

The mistakes of too many past administrations have not doomed Haiti to a state of disrepair. The tired, old bureaucracy is giving way to a pulse of energy generated by throngs of boisterous new leaders. They have the potential to crystalize our people's resolve and bonds—bonds that were and remain a powerful political force. These bonds have also come to define my sense of purpose in life.

Every country relies on its economic infrastructure and standardized practices in order to create a foundation for businesses to thrive. Nations around us dedicate massive resources to develop their human capital through education and social programs. Haiti too is capable of all this and so much more.

Haiti's future growth must be associated with significant financial, institutional and governance reforms reflective of a country that is ripe for economic, social and moral leadership in the world. Our sustainable growth rests in leveling the playing field for everyone, in eradicating corruption through fervent and effective measures and in revamping the entire system to inspire this generation and future ones toward a free, just and peaceful country maintained by a

Constitution adaptive enough to accommodate our collective ambitions.

I believe in the power of storytelling. For that reason, this book reads in part like a memoir and as a historical chapter. In other parts, it is a forward-thinking manifesto, not based merely on passion but pragmatism. My dream of a bright and prosperous Haiti endorses a better form of leadership that protects, promotes and provides hope in order to escape the crippling era of pessimism. That vision of a better country certifies an empowered middle class, effective government and equitable rule of law for a society of peace, security and prosperity.

Our transformation will not be spontaneous, as it requires grassroots efforts involving the full integration of the diaspora with those living at home banding together to enable national conditions that decode into effective and sustainable change. The time has come for us to access the real strength of our diaspora, our generations of educated and highly skilled nationals living and working abroad to advance other nations' economies and social welfare, harnessed into a major source of development financing, a partner for long-term trade and investment through a comprehensive and strategic plan.

We must act *now*—not just to save Haiti but to secure its rightful place in the world through a collective movement to address our most pressing needs and close the gap between government, private industries and the people.

I call upon this dynamic new generation to work together to help Haiti prosper through ethical business traditions, a powerful form of government established on transparency, accountability and strength, with a legacy of strong and engaged citizens—a country in which we can all succeed if we try.

Let us be poised to carry out this mission, that our courage, determination and resources be aligned and befit the task at hand. This should be both an individual and collective mission as we responsibly raise and empower our youth to take charge of their own future and that of the country. It is our duty to fight the burden of leadership deficit left over from previous administrations. It is our obligation to tackle the long-term ramifications of our misfortunes, redesigning our communities to triumph over hardships.

Lastly, we ought to assert authority over chance and fate to underwrite a positive change in the nation's destiny, awakening in the national conscience: a sustainable future full of hope, possibilities and opportunities—*a better Haiti for all*. My call to action is not a reverberation from the past. It is an appeal to my generation's patriotism, rationalism and sense of unity to commit not just their frustrations but also their dexterities, passions and resources toward rebuilding a nation worthy of the next generations' ideals.

This *is the weight of my dream.*

ENDNOTES

Page 45—Hershovitz, Scott (2003), "Legitimacy,
Democracy, and Razian Authority," Legal
Theory, 9: 201–220. Lipset, Seymour Martin
(1959), "Some Social Requisites of Democracy:
Economic Development and Political
Legitimacy," *The American Political Science Review*,
vol. 53, no. 1, pp. 69–105.

Page 47—Hurwitz, Leon (1973), "Contemporary
Approaches to Political Stability," *Comparative
Politics*, vol. 5, no. 3, 1973, pp. 449–63.

Page 47—Eckstein, Harry (1992), *Regarding Politics:
Essays on Political Theory, Stability, and Change,*
University of California Press, retrieved from
http://ark.cdllb.org/ark:/13030/ftOk40037v/

Page 48—Locke, John (1690), *Second Treatise on
Civil Government*, edited by C. B. MacPherson,
Indianapolis: Hackett, 1990. Hobbes, Thomas
(1668), *Leviathan*, edited by Edwin Curley,
Indianapolis: Hackett, 1994.

Page 50—Lijphart, Arend (1977), *Democracy in Plural Societies: A Comparative Exploration*, Yale University Press, New Haven and London.

Page 94—Jonathan M. Katz (2013), *The Big Truck: How the World Came to Save Haiti and Left a Disaster Behind*, St. Martin's Press, New York.

Page 107—Adam Smith (1776), *The Wealth of Nations*, Penguin Classics, 1982, Penguin Random House, New York and London.

REFERENCES

Buss, T. F., & Gardner, A. (2008). *Haiti in the balance, Why Foreign Aid has failed and what we can do about it.* Washington: The Brooking Institution.

Development and Cooperation EuropeAid. (2014). *Evaluation of EU Cooperation with the Republic of Haiti, 2008-2012.* Freiburg.

Engaging the Haitian Diaspora—The Cairo Review of Global . . . https://www.thecairoreview.com/essays/engaging-the-haitian-diaspora/

Fund for Peace. (2019). *Fragile State Index, 2019.* Washington: Fund for Peace. Retrieved from https://fragilestatesindex.org/country-data/

Global Affairs Canada. (2015). *Evaluation of Canada-Haiti Cooperation, 2006-2013.* Ottawa: Global Affairs Canada. Retrieved from https://www.international.gc.ca/gac-amc/publications/evaluation/2015/dev-eval-canada-haiti01.aspx?lang=eng#toc_3_5

Held, David, 1995. *Democracy and the Global Order,* Paolo Alto: Stanford University Press.——, 2002. "Law of States, Law of Peoples: Three Models of Sovereignty," *Legal Theory* 8(1):1–44.

IMF Country Report No. 13/91 HAITI. https://www.imf.org/external/pubs/ft/scr/2013/cr1391.pdf

Inter-American Development Bank. (2011). *Country Program Evaluation, 2007-2011.* Inter-American Development Bank.

International Bank for Reconstruction and Development. (1995). *Consultative Group for Haiti report.* Retrieved from "The objective was to designate donors to each of the Haiti's sectoral priorities."

International Monetary Fund (2018). *Pursuing Women's Economic Empowerment* https://www.imf.org/en/Publications/Policy-Papers/Issues/2018/05/31/pp053118pursuing-womens-economic-empowerment

Kulendran, N. & Kenneth Wilson (2000) Is there a relationship between international trade and international travel? *Applied Economics,* 32:8, 1001-1009, DOI: 10.1080/000368400322057

Milne, Simon & Irena Ateljevic (2001) Tourism, economic development and the global-local nexus: Theory embracing complexity, *Tourism Geographies*, 3:4, 369-393, DOI: 10.1080/146166800110070478

Mishra P., Rout H.B., Mohapatra S.S. Causality between tourism and economic growth: Empirical evidence from India. Eur. J. Soc. Sci. 2011;18:518–527

OECD. (2008). *The Paris Declaration on Aid Effectiveness and the Accra Agenda for Action*. OECD. Retrieved from http://www.oecd.org/dac/effectiveness/34428351.pdf

OECD. (2009). *Monitoring the Fragile States Principles: Reflections on Issues of Capacity and Capacity Development*. OECD. Retrieved from https://www.oecd.org/countries/democraticrepublicofthecongo/45343232.pdf

OECD; Canadian International Development Agency. (2010). *Monitoring the Principles for Good International Engagement in Fragile States and Situations, Case of Haiti*. OECD. Retrieved from www.oecd.org/countries/haiti/45600837.pdf

OECD. (2019). *Development Aid at a glance: America.* OECD. Retrieved from https://www.oecd.org/dac/financing-sustainable-development/development-finance-data/America-Development-Aid-at-a-Glance-2019.pdf

Outline for Report on the—OAS. https://www.cidh.oas.org/countryrep/HAITI%20 ENGLISH7X10%20FINAL.pdf

Selznick, Philip (1957). *Leadership in Administration.* New York, NY: Harper & Row.

Sengupta, Chandan (2004) "Political and Social Stability: Ideas, Paradoxes and Prospects." *Economic and Political Weekly*, vol. 39, no. 48, 2004, pp. 5101–5105.

The role of political party finance reform in the https://www.u4.no/publications/the-role-of-political-party-finance-reform-in-the-transition-from-dominant-to-competitive-party-systems

UNDP. (2018). *Human Development Indices and Indicators.* New York: UNDP. Retrieved from http://www.hdr.undp.org/sites/default/files/2018_human_development_statistical_update.pdf

UNI-WIDER. (2014). *Aid Failures in Haiti: Exploring the Fatal Flaw.* Helsinki: UNI-WIDER.

UN Secretary General's High Level Panel on Women's Economic Empowerment, Leave No One Behind: A Call to Action for Gender Equality and Women's Economic Empowerment. Available at: https://www.empowerwomen. org/-/media/files/un%20women/empower-women/resources/hlp%20briefs/unhlp%20 full%20report.pdf?la=en

UN Women, *Turning Promises into Action: Gender Equality in the 2030 Agenda for Sustainable Development* (New York, 2018). Available at: https://www.unwomen.org/en/digital-library/publications/2018/2/gender-equality-in-the-2030-agenda-for-sustainable-development-2018

Western Union, "Western Union Pays Tribute to Global Women Work-Force as World Economic Change Agents and Calls for Greater Recognition and Integration", 8 March 2016. Available at: http://ir.western-nunion.com/news/archived-press-releases/

press-release-details/2016/Western-Union-Pays-
Tribute-to-Global-Women-Work-Force-as-
World-Economic-Change-Agents-and-Calls-
for-Greater-Recognition-and-Integration/
default.aspx

World Bank, Independent Evaluation Group. (2015).
CLR Review, Haiti. World Bank. World Bank.

ACKNOWLEDGMENTS

Writing this book was a great life experience all on its own. As for every other milestone added to my life journey, glory be to the Almighty!

There has been a congregation of exceptional people who helped me along the way.

To my good friend, Jacques Remarais, who encouraged me to document my dreams and experience, thank you. But this volume could not have been written without the unique impetus of the indefatigable Nora A. Gay, who provided me with the unconditional support necessary to complete it. From the bottom of my heart, thank you very much for your sacred dedication to me.

I must express my earnest gratitude to Wedline for fulfilling the parenting commitments that require physical proximity when my career path and endless traveling saddened our children. To my incredibly encouraging family, particularly my brothers, Dr. Jacobsen Saint Victor and Rolf, my sister Dapheline and my daughter Amy for their emotional sustenance throughout the writing process, thank you all for always having my back.

Huge thanks to Rose Marie Théard and my band of brothers whose constant spiritual support enhanced my vigilance and growth on the path to finding answers for Haiti: Brother Jude Cherie, Brother Jean Remy Sandeus, Brother Voltaire Pamphile, Brother Yves Dambreville, Brother Féliton Augustin, Brother Adolphe Mezadieu, Brother Raphael Alexandre, Brother Richardson Chavré, Brother Frantz Bastien, Brother Antonio Balan, Brother Milord Souffrant and Brother Emmanuel Maceus.

To Mayor Will Flanagan, Perry Long, Shawn Cadime, Steve Torres and all the individuals I have had the opportunity to work with in Fall River government and to my long list of friends and political associates in New Bedford, Massachusetts: Lisa Lemieux, Dana Rebeiro, Steven Martins, Joe Lopes, Timothy Klatt, Donald Rei, Josh Amaral, Brian Gomes, Richard Porteus Jr. and Will Gardner, whose influence inspired me, thank you all for being part of my foundation.

I will forever be indebted to Stephane Vincent, Sandy Baptiste and Steeve Moliere Noel, who helped me move back to Haiti and connected me to a network of people who shared their gifts and mentored me. I am very fortunate for all the great friends I have made while living in Haiti. To Naikema Nicolas, Ruth Marc, Djenane Desrouleaux, Christine Jacques, Nancy Carraha, Laurette Backer, Esther Antoine, Gaimcy François, Emmanuel Jean-François, Renald Luberice, Thierry Pierre-Louis, Junior Salomon, Calvin Cadet, Daniel Joseph, Shiller Torchon, Gary Bernadotte, Jeffsky Poincy, Websder Corneille, Ernso

Pierre, Michael Stitt, Diego Gouin, Alex Jacques, Rooloph René, and many more, thank you for always rooting for me.

Life in Haiti has its shares of privation. Some days were better because of the guardian angels sent my way to teach and aid me indispensably. I am most grateful to Georges Nader Jr., whose compassion and understanding extended a worthy tenant credit line, allowing me never to go homeless. A boundless appreciation for Magalie Latortue, who taught me how to harness my hidden gifts, overcome the forces of this world and triumph over the unknown. Heartfelt thanks to Clara Rigaud for having added value to my life in her way.

Thanks to everyone on the publishing and editing team: Gary M. Krebs, Randy Ladenheim-Gil, two excellent editors whose thoughtful review and suggestions were imperative, and Libby Kingsbury, one of the best designers I've ever met. Lastly, I am eternally grateful to everyone who reads this book.